Uncle George
& Company

Uncle George & Company

Humphrey Phelps

ALAN SUTTON
1984

Alan Sutton Publishing Limited
Brunswick Road · Gloucester

First published 1984

British Library Cataloguing in Publication Data

Phelps, Humphrey
Uncle George and company.
1. Country life—England—Gloucestershire
—History—20th century 2. Gloucestershire
—Social life and customs
I. Title
942.4'1083   DA670.G5

ISBN 0-86299-139-0

Typesetting and origination by
Alan Sutton Publishing Limited
Photoset Plantin 11/12
Printed in Great Britain

For my grandson Harley,
some years hence

Contents

Chapter One

The Garden Shed

For me the shed was a source of delight; it stood in a corner of the garden and was covered in honeysuckle. A high wall formed two of its sides, the rest of it was constructed of old railway sleepers, weather boarding and corrugated iron. It was, I suppose, a ramshackle affair, over the years it had been extended again and again, making it in effect a series of caverns; each succeeding cavern more dusky and mysterious than the preceding one. In those dusky interiors with their strange aroma compounded of cider, onions, blood and bone meal, the fustiness of damp earth, old sacks, and Lord knows what else; among the garden tools, barrels of cider, bottles of home-made wine, strings of onions, bunches of seaweed, the flower pots, old chairs, the oil stove, mugs and jugs, wooden chests, sacks and boxes, one never knew what one might find. But mostly I found delight and magic; riches beyond the reach of money.

The shed belonged to Uncle George, my father's elder brother. They were devoted to each other but in appearance and manner they were very different. Father was of small wiry stature, always tidily dressed, quiet and unobtrusive, keeping himself to himself. George was large and fat; invariably wearing old and tattered clothes and with a spotted red handkerchief tied round his neck. George was rumbustic, dogmatic, a man who spread himself around, and with a deep rumbling voice. There was a magical quality about him; in a twinkling of an eye, with an expansive smile, a broad wink or a grimace and a gesture with his huge hands he could and frequently did turn everything to merriment. From his ruddy, and usually unshaven, face would come great gusts of laughter which took control and shook his huge bulk. He could be very solemn, pompous or bombastic, but I never knew if these attitudes were real or assumed. Despite his age he retained a child's sense of wonder and optimism and a fund of mischief.

It was here in this shed that Uncle George pondered upon the strange ways of the world and men and the stranger, unfathomable ways of women – he was I should explain a bachelor and rather wary of women in general. Or he spent his time thinking of new schemes or even newer schemes when the earlier ones went awry as they sometimes did. He always seemed rather perplexed about the failure of his plans to which he gave such careful thought. But never downhearted, or at least not for long, there was a kind of effervescence about him and as he often said, 'You can't keep a good man down.' I had no doubts who the good man was, and neither for that matter had Uncle George.

Mother had no doubts about him either, she held several and decided opinions about Uncle George, but not one of them could possibly be interpreted as good. Mother valued respectability and all the conventions of those who aspire to being middle-class, who must have people to look up to and people to look down upon. Uncle, with careless or perhaps studied abandon, violated all the rules of polite society and she regarded him as a shameless reprobate, a disgrace to the family, a bad influence all round, but a particularly bad influence on me. She called him a dirty, disgusting man, a horrible man who would be the ruination of me and the death of her. She particularly disapproved of the way he dressed; the handkerchief round his neck, his stained and shabby corduroy trousers, his drinking and gossiping. To make matters worse he was a frequent visitor to our house and his visits were welcomed by both father and me.

'Time our George was here,' Father often said after he had closed his hardware shop and had his tea. 'Is he coming again tonight, the cratur's here every whipstitch,' Mother would say. 'If he starts talking about murder and scandal and illnesses tonight, I shall put my hat and coat on and go – I just can't stand any more of it.'

'I thought he would look in.'

'On his way to that wretched Lion to drink himself silly as usual. I cannot stand another dose of him tonight, he's here every Sunday for dinner, filling his great canister and squatting here for most of the afternoon, talking about the scandals in the *News of the World*, and making nasty noises. It's never fit, it's never fit.'

Uncle George had a wide variety of interests, but they were

mainly centred around pigs, gardening, scandals and gossip local and national, murders, illness, doctors and patent medicines. He could discourse upon murders for hours, recalling notorious murders of the past and speculating upon recent ones, he would talk about well known detectives, pathologists and barristers as though they were personal friends of his. Illness seemed to fascinate him and when the mood took him he would become eloquent and knowledgeable about them. Nasty, morbid and unwholesome, Mother would call it. From his conversation it appeared that he knew all the local doctors and those at the hospital in our market town. Those that were 'clever men' and those that were 'no bottle'. Sometimes a specialist at the hospital would capture his approbation and he would call him 'a coming man'.

'Yes,' he would say, assuming his solemn, judicial manner, 'he's a coming man, you just wait and see if he ain't, he's a coming man an' he'll soon be gone, it won't be long afore he's in Harley Street, soak me bob if he ain't. I've a durned good mind to go an' see him afore he's gone.'

Uncle George paid frequent visits to Dr Higgins' surgery in the village. 'Higgins is a good old stick. Not clever mind, but sound. I've got respect for Higgins although he can't fathom what's the matter with me.'

Mother said there was nothing the matter with him except greed, drink, idleness, a nasty mind and disgusting habits and that any ailments he might have were self inflicted.

Uncle George was also a great believer in patent medicines – he avidly read the advertisements in the papers.

'See this,' he would say, producing a cutting from his waistcoat pocket, 'this seems to be some useful stuff, just the stuff I need for my little complaint. Look, they speak very highly of it – here 'tis in black an' white, don't know why Higgins don't get a stock on't in. Perhaps he will when I tell him about it. But I don't expect he will, I've told him about stuff afore and he ain't ever took no notice. They don't like bein' told y'know, these doctors don't, they be funny like that. 'Tis a pity though, 'cos I could put 'em on to some good stuff that 'ould do some good. D'you know, I heard of some master stuff once an' I put meself out – an' I was pertickler busy at the time – to go out of me way – an' how I was placed at the time I could ill afford the time, but I went special down to Higgins to tell him. An' 'pon my soul, you'll hardly credit this, j'you know what he said, he said "George, don't try and teach yer grandmother to suck eggs." That's what he said. That's the thanks you get when you try to do a man a good turn. Course, they likes to mix up their own stuff, that's what's behind it, but when he's stumped, I shouldn't wonder if he don't get some of the stuff I've told'n about an' put it in his own bottles an' packets – well, you con't blame him if he do. Still, it 'ould be nice if he'd show a bit o' gratitude occasionally – if only he'd say, "George, that were some good stuff you put me on to." But there again, I expect he's more or less got to keep mum about it, t'other doctors 'ould get nasty if they got to know as Higgins were relyin' on me for advice – but, mind you, I'd do the same for them.'

He was, I must admit, apt to get over enthusiastic about patent medicines, especially ones he had just discovered. Experience did not dull his enthusiasm or his optimism – his house was littered with bottles and packets of discarded stuff which had once been proclaimed as 'little short of miraculous'. But while the enthusiasm was upon him he could not understand why Dr Higgins or any other doctor 'did not make the utmost use on't.'

'Rubbish,' Mother would say later. 'The rubbish that man talks. And the rubbish he pokes in to that great stomach of his, with all the stuff in there the wonder is that he doesn't explode. If he stopped taking all that stuff and didn't eat and drink so much he may not be so objectionable about the place.'

According to Mother, most of Uncle George's opinions and pronouncements were rubbish except those that we downright nasty, wicked, malicious or untrue such as his frequent references to Mrs Peabody, Mother's friend, and her secret meetings with a man in the spinney. 'It's not true, it's not true. Mrs Peabody is a respectable married woman, she plays the organ at church.' Father's stock answer, 'Sure to be right, if our George says so,' though spoken in smoothing tones did nothing to smooth Mother's wrath and indignation. And to which she would rejoin, 'He only says it because Mrs Peabody's my friend.'

Uncle George was a smallholder by inclination, but a baker by trade, having inherited the bakery from his father. I don't think he disliked the business, provided he could get someone else to light the bakehouse fire, mix the dough, put it into tins, bake the bread and look after the shop; and as long as he could ignore the book-keeping. 'But,' as he said, 'a man as do love pigs an' gardenin' don't want messin' about with bread.'

'People,' said Mother, 'do not like bread made and delivered by a man who always smells of pigs, and a man with the habits of a pig, who never shaves and has a filthy bit of rag round his neck. And who, as like as not won't bother to deliver it if he isn't in the mood. If only he cleaned himself up and paid more attention to the business instead of poking his nose into other people's business, everybody would be a lot healthier and happier and so would his business. Fancy delivering bread with your clothes and boots covered in pig muck, people don't fancy it either, no more do they like it when he doesn't bother to deliver bread. And to think that such a man is my brother-in-law, it makes me so ashamed. And he uses words and expressions that would never have passed my father's lips. If my father were alive and could hear what I've heard from that man, he'd turn in his grave.'

Uncle George had an orchard where his Saddleback and Gloucester Old Spot pigs roamed, where he kept his hens, sheep and his bee hives. The pigs ate the grass and the fallen fruit, the sheep grazed, the hens ate insects which might otherwise have harmed his trees, and pigs, sheep and hens helped to fertilise the land while the bees helped to pollenate the trees. But when pigs, sheep, hens and hives of bees mixed the result was pandemonium.

At the bottom of the orchard stood a few buildings, including the cider house. In the autumn, with the assistance of his two friends, Reuben and Colonel, Uncle George made cider. Throughout the year, again with the assistance of Reuben and Colonel, he drank cider in that cool, dark, fragrant place. Colonel was colonel in name only, no one could remember how he'd come by the name, but everyone called him 'Colonel' except Mother, who referred to him as 'that man Biggs.' He and Reuben made a precarious living by doing odd jobs, supplemented by a little poaching and other doubtful activities. Father called them likeable rascals, Mother called them drunken rogues or a couple of ne'er do wells. Uncle George called them good chaps, useful fellas and damn good company. Most of the time, but occasionally their relationship would be strained; perhaps because of a difference of opinion, because they had done something to displease him or because they failed to turn up when they were needed. They were both given to failing to turn up, to making promises which they never kept – 'dabsters at the game' as Uncle George put it. But they didn't often practice their game with him, they liked Uncle George's cider too much. When they were out of favour with Uncle he called them 'muntles', 'gutsy baggers' and 'low bred varmints'.

The cider house with its barrels was almost as exciting as the garden shed and so were the adjoining buildings which housed the pigs, the stable with horse and harness; and the loft with hay where hens laid eggs. Sometimes a dozen or more eggs would be discovered in a nest, but once discovered the nest would be abandoned. 'Drat they hens,' Uncle would mutter, but it was exciting searching for new nests and clutches of eggs I thought. In another shed there were shelves with innumerable bottles and packets of animal medicine; drenches and ointments for horses, cattle, sheep and pigs; warble fly dressings, sheep dip, footrot ointment, worming powders, pig powders, poultry spice, glauber's salts, rock salts and minerals.

Uncle George's house, garden, orchard and buildings lay just outside the village, some little distance from the bakery which was in the High Street. The bakery was also an exciting place, especially early in the mornings with the glowing oven, the sparks from the ashes when the fire was raked out, the smell of wood smoke, yeast and freshly baked bread.

In the bakery yard were bundles of faggots which harboured rats; on some Sunday afternoons, Uncle George, assisted by Reuben and his terriers, would decide to 'rout out they damn rats'. To the annoyance of Mrs Peabody who lived next to the yard. 'Have you no respect for the Sabbath,' she would scream from the other side of the wall. 'And you'll disturb my husband with all the noise you are making. He's having a nap, my husband is.'

'The bagger's too drunk to be disturbed, I'll warrant,' Uncle would mutter.

After the rat hunt, we would go into the dusty, gloomy office for a mug of cider, because as Uncle always observed, 'rat huntin' is devilish thirsty work'. Come to think of it, all the activities of Uncle's, or Reuben's or Colonel's for that matter, were 'devilish, thirsty work'. One could easily see from the amount of dust in that office and the thick layers of it on the ledgers that any work connected with book-keeping would be 'devilish thirsty work'. But Uncle ignored accounts as much as he could. 'Drat 'em, an' drat them as thinks I've got nothin' better to do than muddle with accounts,' grumbled Uncle from time to time. 'I'll do 'em one day, when I ain't got nothin' better to do. But when that'll be I don't know.' Adding after a pause, 'An' I don't bloody well care either.'

He could not have been short of money, he must have settled his accounts, at least I never heard of his being in any bother about owing money. Of course he was paid in cash each week by most of his customers, others had monthly accounts, but he rarely bothered to render accounts to those who were, as he put it, 'all right'. Many of those who were 'all right' waited years before receiving accounts. If they persisted in asking for an account it was likely to cause offence and the remark: 'Dussent kip worryin' me for accounts, I be far too busy just now. Just thee bide a while and stop frettin', thee'll get one all in good time.'

Even in those pre-war days, his shop would have been considered old fashioned. 'No fal-de-lals here. 'Twas good enough for my father an' what was good enough for him is good enough for me. Mebbe a lick o' paint yur an' thur wouldn't come amiss some day when ol' Reuben and me 'ave the time to spare, but I ain't 'avin' that ol' Sam to do't an' that's a fact.' Sam was his brother-in-law, his sister Aggie's husband, and a lank, dour fellow. 'He ain't no bottle, old Sam, but our Aggie do seem to like'n.'

Uncle did not care for shop work and avoided it as much as he could, leaving a boy in charge of the shop while he went out delivering bread with the horse and van. And if he had no one to look after the shop, he simply shut it up if other business called him away or he was not in the mood to stand behind the counter. Notices were sometimes hung on the door: SOW FARROWING, or BACK IN AN HOUR – URGENT BUSINESS. Even Father admitted it was no way to conduct a business; Mother said it was disgraceful. Occasionally Colonel was called upon to do duty in the shop, but as Uncle said, 'Old Colonel ain't what I'd call a fust class chap behind the counter.'

Although the shop stocked various other items, such as packets of flour and biscuits, tea, eggs, cheese and a few cakes – Uncle was very proud of his doughnuts and lardy cakes –

some tinned food, yeast, and produce from his orchard and garden, once the bread was sold, or almost all sold, the shop was closed.

'That's it for today, lock the door,' Uncle said to the boy who served in the shop, 'I ain't payin' you to hang about yer – if you want to earn another bob or two I can find you a job down at my place for an hour or so. And I want to get off, none of 'em can want anythin' very badly or they'd a bin yer afore now. An' if there is any bread about I can take it out on the round today or tomorrow. In any case new bread ain't any good to you, it do give you the wind. Slip the bolt across an' get from yer. Out the back way mind, don't let anybody see you goin'. 'Tis a wonderful funny thing, you've only got to shut the front door an' the baggers start 'ammerin' an' clamourin' for stuff. An' if they see you leavin' the shop they start 'ollerin'.'

Usually the door was closed at about half past one and Uncle would creep out furtively from the yard at the back of the shop and then scamper off home or into the White Lion. He had even been known to close the shop when trade was still comparatively brisk, at least once when it was very brisk. 'I ain't puttin' up with any more o' this,' he announced upon that occasion. 'You've had all mornin' to get what you do want; now if you want bread or cake or summat get it quick an' be gone. I've had enough on't for one day an' I'm closin' in five minutes an' if King Peter comes 'ammerin' on that door when the bolt's across, 'e can 'ammer 'til 'e's blue in the face.'

Mother often recalled that occasion, but as Father said, 'Our George has got bread to deliver in the afternoon, they can't expect him to hang about.' But secretly, I suspect, Father did not approve of his brother's attitude. Uncle's shop which was comparatively bare – except for the many old calendars going back for decades and still hanging on the walls; Father's shop was cluttered with tools, saucepans, kettles, pots and pans, poultry and dog food, garden seeds and fertilisers, lamps, fencing wire and ironmongery. And Father would never dream of closing his shop until the proper time, nor neglecting the accounts. 'Pemberthy,' Father did observe from time to time, 'will take all our George's trade if our George don't look out, but of course he can't bake bread.' Pemberthy kept the general stores; he had only been in the village a few years and was a keener business man than the other local shopkeepers. 'A thruster,' Uncle George called him and the tone in which he said it implied that Pemberthy was not to be entirely trusted. As Pemberthy was a newcomer, it was an opinion that was held by many of the local people; in Pemberthy's shop people counted their change very carefully. Pemberthy himself was partly the cause of suspicion, he regarded himself and even boasted that he was astute. And, reasoned the local people, if being astute did not mean trying to take advantage of other people, what did it mean?

Watch Pemberthy they said and watch Pemberthy they did; and, in the main, they preferred Uncle George's lackadaisical ways to the more business-like and obliging ways of Pemberthy. In any case, Uncle George was a local man, the older people remembered his father and grandfather – you knew where you were with a local man. As a matter of fact, they did not always know where they were with Uncle George, nobody did, not even Uncle himself. But Uncle was a local man and a local man's peccadiloes may be criticised, but sooner or later are overlooked. Not by everybody of course, a man who gossiped and interfered in other people's business as much as Uncle did was bound to have enemies and Uncle had a few.

Micah Elford, the fishmonger and greengrocer, whose property was next to Uncle's orchard, was one. He and Uncle were continually at loggerheads and they would have ceased to be on speaking terms long ago had they not found so much pleasure in shouting abuse at each other. Uncle George hated, or pretended to hate perhaps, the man who was the cause of so much enjoyment to him, but I think he liked Micah's wife. 'Poor little 'oman, she've got a lot to put up with; all that stinkin' old fish and Micah's nasty ways. My heart do bleed for that poor 'oman, Micah's that mean, 'e wunt even put her a decent W.C. I've sin that poor 'oman goin' down the garden path in all winds and weathers to that broken down old place, all the boards off the back lettin' the wind blow up an' the door off its hinges. It's a wonder 'er don't have somethin' come to 'er poor 'oman. If 'tweren't for 'er sake, I'd report that ol' Micah an' 'is stinkin' ol' fish an' drains to the nuisance man.'

Micah delivered fish round the district in a motor van. Occasionally he and Uncle George in the baker's van would meet in the narrow lanes and neither would be disposed to draw into the verge to allow the other to pass.

'Git in the side, Micah, 'oot!'

'Pull thic 'oss aside, George.'

'I'll be durned if I will. Hosses 'ave the right of way.'

And Uncle invariably did make Micah give way. I think he looked forward to these chance encounters with his old enemy; he certainly enjoyed delivering bread more than anything else connected with the bakery business although it meant being out 'in all winds and weathers and at all hours of the day and night'. If often was 'all hours of the day and night' too, he was called the midnight baker. But this was his own fault; he would stop and talk and gossip with his favourite customers, sometimes for hours, especially if they gave him cups of tea, cider, home-made wine, or some interesting news, gossip or scandal which would then have to be told to more of his customers in turn and which gained more detail with each subsequent recital. Pigs, gardens and orchards had to be inspected and lengthy advice given. 'Them pigs need worming . . .' 'Powders, give 'em powders . . .' Tips on how to grow 'master onions' and other vegetables, on pruning and how to avoid pests and diseases – 'pig's muck's the stuff, you can't beat pig muck in the orchard – plaster it on an' you wunt be troubled by pests an' suchlike an' you'll get some master crops, damn my rags if you wunt.' He was an acknowledged authority on fruit and vegetable growing and took most of the prizes at our annual show.

The virtues of his patent medicines would be extolled: 'I can put you on to the very stuff for your little trouble . . .' 'Thur's nothing like charcoal tablets to help you with the wind. I wouldn't be without them.' 'New bread's no good for you, that's why I allus kip a few loaves back for my friends. Old bread but fresh fish I allus say. Stinkin' ol' fish can be lethal.'

When I went with Uncle George in the baker's van, he'd say, 'Here you are, boy, you take over now,' and hand me the reins. This was the moment I had been waiting for from the time we had got into the van; to hold the reins and to be seen holding the reins by everyone we met. 'An' don't ferget, boy, you've got the right of way, let them motors pull aside and draw up.' He always called me 'boy' but treated me as a man; boys may be boys but they like to be thought of and treated as men. Uncle knew everyone we saw and everyone knew him, it was wonderful that anyone could know and be known to so many people and no less wonderful to be the nephew of such a man. He knew every field and garden, all that had happened in them and what would happen. He stopped to chat to the men in the fields by the roads, bellowed greetings to those in distant fields – in those days men could still be seen working in fields. If we came to a pub that was open, he dismounted for 'a quick one' and bought me a glass of lemonade 'to wet your whistle.'

Then there were the customers, the ones who were jolly and those who were miserable. Some just said, 'Where did you get to last time, George?' Some complained and others just laughed. Some gave me cake or sweets, but a few rather frightened me. But, as Uncle said, 'you must take 'em as you find 'em.' And on those days when I took the reins I found the world a wonderful and rather exciting place. At any moment we might meet Micah. 'Hey there, Micah. Pull in, thur's a gurt ditch my side. Pull in an' let us get by quickly. My hoss can't stand the smell of stinkin' ol' fish.'

Just around the next corner adventure or comedy might be lurking, or men with lurid stories to tell, or strange happenings or characters larger than life. On our homeward journey we might see Mrs Peabody walking across a field. 'Thur she goes, off to meet her chap in the spinney.' In Uncle George's company anything might happen. It was a wonderful world.

Chapter Two

The Man Who Swallowed a Wheelbarrow

The bees were still busy in the lime tree, and the air redolent of lime blossom and honeysuckle. It had been a hot and sultry day but now, as the sun dipped towards the rim of the hill, casting its long rays over the garden, the heat abated. Uncle George put his wheelbarrow down and sat on an upturned fruit box. 'Phew!' he exclaimed, 'I'm sweatin' like a bull, it's bin a hot un today an' no mistake.' He mopped his face and ran a finger round the inside of the handkerchief round his neck. 'Don't just stand there, boy, go an' get a mug of cider out of the shed.'

As I moved towards the garden shed, he shouted, 'Not out o' the fust cask, get it outa the second un. I be a savin' that out o' the fust un for old Colonel, it chun't very good, it 'ave gone off a bit, but 'tis good enough fer that ol' nogman, he'll swaller anythin'.' I was in the shed now, but I could still hear Uncle George rumbling away. 'Of course, he don't taste it, he's that gutsy, he just pours it down like water goin' down a drain. Cider's all right as long as you don't abuse it. Drink, drink for thy stomach's sake, but don't yut to kill thyself I do allus say, but that ain't no reason to make a pig of yerself. . . .'

Uncle was lighting his pipe when I returned. 'Cider's all right in moderation,' said Uncle when he'd got his pipe going well, 'but old Colonel don't understand the meaning of the word.' He took his pipe from his mouth and started sniffing.

'Can you smell anything?' he asked.

'Your tobacco, the lime and honeysuckle.'

'No, no, not that. I thought I caught a whiff of fish, roarin', stinkin' ol' fish from over at that old Micah's. Just a whiff mind, but 'tis some distance so't must be fair roarin' if I caught even a whiff on't. Mind you, even if I didn't, but I'm sure I did – you sure you didn't? – perhaps 'twas worst when you was still in the shed. There ain't no breeze to send it this way, thank the Lord, but the whiff I had fair roared. As it would this weather, bin hangin' about for days, I expect, and it would whiffle. He'll never have the neck to hawk that about on his round tomorrow, will he? But he will, he won't throw anythin' away, he's too mean to do that.'

Uncle paused and rubbed his chin, which caused a rasping sound, before continuing, 'Of course, I might have imagined it, the trouble is that stinkin' ol' fish is playin' on my mind. When I passed his shop today 'twas enough to knock you back.' Uncle, I thought, had probably had another row with Micah.

'I wonder where that ol' Colonel is, he promised faithfully to give me a bit of a hand today. That's the trouble with chaps today, they be got so unreliable. I don't know why I bother with that ol' muntle, the way he goes on. I tell you, boy, 'tis no way to go on, no way at all. An' I've been damn good to the old fool, it's downright ungrateful the way he treats me. But never mind, no more cider for him. Reuben, I shall say when I see 'em together, you be welcome to as much of my beautiful cider as you do want, but not another drop for Colonel, not another drop.'

I knew from past experience that tomorrow or the next day Colonel would be here or in the cider house with a mug in his hand and Uncle would be saying to him, 'Drink, drink, for thy stomach's sake.'

After I had re-filled the mug Uncle pointed to the wheelbarrow and said, 'You don't see many wheelbarrows of that quality about today. You couldn't buy one like that today for love nor money. Your father have got some fairish barrows in stock, but they byunt a patch on that un. That's a prince among barrows that is, made by a master craftsman.'

To emphasise his words, and so that there could be no possible doubt which wheelbarrow he was talking about, he picked up his stick and prodded the barrow. 'Old Edgar Bailey was a tradesman and he made that barrow.' We gazed at the wheelbarrow in silent appreciation for some time while innumerable bees murmured in the lime tree.

'Yes,' said Uncle, tapping out his pipe on the heel of his leather boot, 'he were a tradesman an' no mistake, and, rajah rhubarb, he could make a good barrow! Soak me bob an' damn my rags if he couldn't. Well, you do know the feel of that barrer there, a joy to 'andle, a pleasure to trundle, the balance on him, the look on him, a barrer fit for King Peter himself, a barrer to be proud on. An' old Edgar Bailey down in the village made him. Gone, gone, these many years, poor old Edgar, there'll never be no more barrers like thic un there, no, never. Poor old Edgar's dead and buried and he'll make no more barrers.'

Uncle gazed at the wheelbarrow and sighed, wrinkled his brow and nose, puffed out his cheeks and then sighed again. A long silence followed.

At last Uncle George emerged from his reverie and with his eyes still fixed on the wheelbarrow said, 'It were just such a summer's night as this as old Tom swallowed the wheelbarrow.'

Now, I'd heard some pretty extraordinary stories from Uncle George but never anything like this. Perhaps I had misheard him, so I asked him what he'd said.

'I said, "'twere just such a night as this as old Tom swallered a wheelbarrow".'

I was amazed, and the amazement must have shown on my face, because he added, 'It were a long time ago,' and in such a tone as if it were quite feasible, even if rare, for men to swallow wheelbarrows years ago. 'Mind,' he said, 'he only did it once, he didn't make a habit of it.'

'Never!'

'Oh, ah, and it were one of Edgar Felix Bailey's barrers too. That's what put me in mind on't, studyin' this barrer yur, and talkin' about Edgar Bailey and the evenin' bein' like the evenin' old Tom did it. But it were a long time ago mind.'

Uncle George refilled his pipe, chuckled and said, 'Would you like me to tell you about the man who swallowed a wheelbarrow?'

'Please, Uncle,' I said.

⋆   ⋆   ⋆   ⋆   ⋆

Well, (said Uncle George) I'll start at the beginning, and by that I mean I'll tell you summat about old Tom fust, the manner o' man he was an' suchlike an' anythin' else as do occur to me as we go along. Old Tom, his full name was Tom Godwin, but some called him Zachary. He were gettin' on a bit at the time of this story, well, he lived a good three miles from here, nearer four I shouldn't wonder, if you had to walk it. Way over yonder, up the hill an' down the dale, turn right at the crossroads an' then left or maybe 'tis right, I forget now, 'tis not a way I go very often, but 'tis no matter. It 'ould come back to me if I went along there, I could take you to the very house he lived in, a little whitewashed place with a slate roof and a tidy sized garden with a couple of paddocks. Lived there for years, old Tom did. Yes, 'twere left and then right an' on along, past the old lime kilns, on the edge of the Forest – up a bit of an old track.

He didn't get down to the village much – not once in a blue moon, but everybody knowed him, he were a mighty man when he were younger by all accounts, into this and into that, all in a very small way of course, he were only a little mighty man. A bit o' dealin' an' suchlike, 'twas the drink as held him back an' got him into a fair few scrapes an' lost his money for him – once started on the bottle he couldn't leave it alone, about like old Colonel. As he got older he quietened down, a nice chap, a nice chap, generous to a fault, everybody liked'n an' there was them as took advantage of his good nature, I'll warrant.

An' when he got a fair drop of pop in him, he'd start singin' 'Tiddley-pom, tiddley-pom,' an' it were hey-up, look-up. Oh, he could swaller all right, just like old Colonel. Except he could go on swallerin' longer than old Colonel can. I hadn't seen him for ages before that night of the barrer business, he'd got as he kept hisself to hisself. Mind you, I knew he were about a barrer although I hadn't seen him – in that respect it were no surprise to see him in the village that night I be speakin' of.

Y'see, I happened to stop an' have a word with Edgar one day – his shop was just behind the church – an' there Edgar was, just finishin' puttin' the finishin' touches to a barrer. Now the funny thing was that only a month or two afore he'd told me that he weren't goin' to make no more barrers, gettin' too old, he said. 'Ho,' I says to him, thought you weren't goin' to make no more wheelbarrows.' 'No more was I,' he says, 'but Tom Godwin, he comes and asks I to make'n one, an' he pleads with me, says he's set his heart on havin' one of my barrers. An' then after a bit he says there's no need for you to worry, I've got the money put by. An' so I says, all right then, Tom, I'll make one for you.'

So I says to Edgar, 'If you can make Tom Godwin a barrer, you can make one for me, I've got my heart set on one too. 'An' Edgar, he says, 'Well, George, since it's you, I'll do't, but it'll be the last I ever make.' An' that's him there, the very last barrer Edgar ever made. That's a barrer, that is, he's a pleasure to handle. Different to them mass produced things. It's the balance y'see. You can tell just by the feel of him as soon as you put yer hands on him that he bent no ordin'ry barrer. There's a good many as have wanted that barrer, there's a fair few that have tried to get'n too, by fair means or foul. Ole Micah for one, an' as you might guess, by pretty dirty, underhand foul means. Oh, he's a coveteous varmint what'll try any mean trick to get what he wants. I bin offered money for that barrer, but the money ain't made yet as 'ould buy that barrer off me. Some 'ave wheedled an' cajoled, some 'ave begged an' implored. Some 'ave almost got on their bended knees to borrer me barrer. Ole Colonel fer one. Now, ask yerself a question, would I be likely to lend me barrer to that drunken ole muntle. God Almighty, what he'd do to'n when he had the drink in him. An' as fer old Micah, he'd bring 'im back stinkin' of ole fish, if he brought 'im back at all which ain't likely.

If you knew all the wiles some of 'em 'ave tried to get that barrer, it 'ould make the tith drop clean out of yer yud, boy. A few years back a stranger come here as nice as you like, all smiles an' fal-de-lals – never set eyes on the chap in me life afore – nice as ninepence he were, an' asked me to lend 'im me barrer to put in a exybitshun. Exybitshun, be damned, I never heard the like on't. As if I was the sort to be 'ad by a trick like that. Never sin the chap afore an' if I'd let him have me barrer, that's the last I'd a sin of 'im or me barrer – not as I wanted to see 'im again mind. An' that ain't all, not by a long chalk, but I'm strayin' from me story – now where was I? I was tellin' you about the man as swallowed the wheelbarrer wasn't I. Did I tell you his name? Tom Godwin it was, he'd got a swaller on 'im, 'tis no wonder when you stop to think on't that he swallered a barrer.

Hold hard, boy, an' don't kip interruptin', it do upset me train o' thought an' me remembrances, it have all gotta come back to me, one by one, just as it happened. If you don't kip quiet it wun't come an' you'll never hear the rights on't. Now, be you listenin', 'cos I be ready to begin at the beginnin'.

It were just such an evenin' as this, just such a day as this, an' just about the same time o' year – damn my rags if it weren't. A hot swelterin' summer's day an' a warmish ole evenin', just such a day as puts a swaller on anybody an' an extra swaller on a chap like Tom Godwin.

Well, I went into the Lion that night, Arnold Ludgater's father kept it then, old Percy Ludgater – Arnold took over when his father died. There was quite a fair little gatherin' in the bar already. An' there, sat in the corner were Tom Godwin. 'Hello, Tom, ole feller,' I says, 'Hellow, Jarge,' he says. 'Fancy seein' you,' I says. 'I just dropped in a bit back,' he says, downin' his beer in fust class style an' callin' for another, an' one for me an' for one an' another, open handed, gen'rous like, which was his manner in a pub. Mind you, some on 'em was makin' a right fuss of him, just to get a free drink; the crafty, scroungin' varmints. 'Real pleased to see you, Tom,' they was sayin'. 'You ain't been here for some time,' said one an' another. 'Have a drink,' Tom kept sayin' to 'em. An' they did. Them what usually had cider was havin' beer, them as usually had halves and made 'em last was havin' pints an' downin' 'em like good uns. 'Ah, just dropped in for a drink,' says old Tom, pleased as a puppy dog on account of bein' made such a fuss on. I were pleased to see 'im and I told him so, but some on 'em was just sayin' it for what they could get, the false craturs.

'He bin here a while,' Percy Ludgater mutters to me, 'an' he ain't half bin a downin' 'em. Just sits there an' I gotta kip takin' 'em to 'im.'

'I ain't half got a swaller on me tonight,' says ole Godwin. 'I believe I could swaller almost anythin'.' An' he did an' all.

'What brought you down here then?' I said.

'Me legs,' said Tom. An' what'll take you back I wondered, the way you be a goin' at it yer legs'll never do't. 'Warmish ole day to walk far unless you got to,' said one. ''Tis a tidy ole step from your place,' said another. 'Ah, 'tis, reckon that's what gave me such a swaller, but I had to come to get me barrer.'

'What barrer,' asked Percy.

'Me new barrer,' said Tom.

'I never seed no barrer,' said Percy.

'I put'n round in your yard out o' sight.'

'New barrer?' asked one.

'Ah,' answered Tom, 'Edgar Bailey 'ave just made'n for me.'

'No, 'e never 'ave!' snapped Percy.

'Never have? Never have?' said Tom. 'Course 'e bloody 'ave an' 'im's out in thy back yard for all to see, although 'im's put round the corner out o' sight.'

'Edgar ain't never makin' no more barrers, he've stopped makin' 'em a while back on account of 'is age an 'is health,' shouted Percy, getting a bit rasty.

'Ah, that's right enough,' said Tom. 'That a true bill, he told me that hisself.'

'Well, there you are then,' said Percy all of a smirk. 'That's what I said. I asked him to make me one and he said he'd finished makin' barrers.'

'That's right,' said Tom.

'Well,' said Percy, gettin' a bit nasty agen – all them Ludgaters be a bit hasty an nasty-like betimes, 'what d'you want comin' in here an' upsettin' everybody for by tellin' 'em he've made you a barrer?'

''Cos he have, 'cos I asked him to,' said Tom, gettin' a bit uppity.

'I asked him too,' said Percy, 'an' he ain't made me one, nor never wunt.'

'P'raps you never asked 'im properly,' said Tom.

'What d'you mean by that?' snapped Percy.

'Oh, tiddley-pom, tiddley-pom,' said ole Tom.

'An' what do that mean?' asked Percy, lookin' really evil by now, 'specially when Colonel and Reuben laughed. There's goin' to be a real barney, I thought to meself, so I thought I'd better do summat.

'Edgar promised to make me a barrer,' I said.

'Oh, he did, did he,' said Percy. 'Seems to me he've bin makin' barrers for everybody 'cept me. Come on, come on, how many of the rest of you baggers here bin pesterin' a poor old man for barrers an' drivin' 'im to his grave. Disgraceful I call it, worritin' a sick man. An' then there's me, I've asked 'im time an' agen for a barrer an' he wunt. Bagger 'is barrers, I 'ouldn't 'ave one of 'is bloody barrers not even if 'e gev me one, not if he axed me on his bended knees, I 'ouldn't.'

There's goin' to be a real ole shindig, a right ole barney if I don't do summat I thought to meself. So I said, 'Bagger barrers.' But that didn't do much good. Percy was glarin', Colonel was gyulin', Tom was uppity-like an' mutterin', 'beautiful barrer'. I had to do summat an' pretty damn quick, soak me bob if I 'adn't, but for once in me life I was stumped. But not for long, I'm never at a loss for long, I can most nearly allus think of summat. An' when I saw Alf Ferris come in I was over to him in a flash. 'Don't ask questions, Alf my boy,' I said, 'but git on that pianner as if yer life depended on't. Anything you like as long as it's jolly an' don't never stop, kip right on an' I'll get you a drink, two if needs be or even three.'

Before you could say Jack Robinson, afore Percy could say anything, Alf had struck up, 'A Little Bit of What You Fancy.' Course, he's a gutsy bagger, do anything for a drink. He don't now of course, 'cos he's jud, but when he was alive he could play a pianner. Soak me bob, he could make a pianner talk. Master chap on a pianner.

'Tiddley-pom-pom, tiddley-pom-pom,' sang Tom.

'Tiddley-pom-pom, my arse,' snorted Percy who then started to sing the words. Percy fancied hisself as a singer – you can see my cunnin' now, gettin' Alf goin' on the pianner. 'Tiddley-pom, tiddley-pom,' sang Tom as the tune ended.

'Sing like a man, sing the proper words,' cried Percy, 'or kip thy mouth shut an' let them as can.'

'Bravo! Bravo, Percy!' I said, 'You sang thic un like a good un.' Percy was a different man, them few words of mine had sweetened 'e no end – as I knew they would.

'Another, another,' cried Percy. 'Let's 'ave another an' all of us'll sing the proper words this time.' He looked across at Tom an' added, 'Those as can.' Alf played an' we all sang 'John Brown's Body'. Tom was singin' the words proper. Percy was singin' and drawin' beer an' sweatin' like a bull. Why, he was even carryin' beer over to Tom.

'I like the good ole rousers,' said Tom, 'but they don't half give you a swaller.'

'Don't you think you've swallowed almost enough, Tom?' I said. 'It's a tidy ole step back to thy place.'

'No, no,' said Tom, as chirpy and as cheery as a chicken, 'not nearly enough. I'm the best judge of when I've had enough.'

There, boy, what do you think of that? Nice way to talk to a feller what 'ave just saved 'im from a barney. 'All as I can say, Tom,' I said, 'is that you aint much of a judge. To my way of thinkin' and judgin' by what I've seen you put away, you've had a sight too much already.'

'Oh, tiddley-pom,' he said.

'Tiddley-pom, be baggered,' I said. 'You'll be tiddley-pom on yer bum afore you gets home, if you ever do get home, the way you bin goin' at it yer 'ead nor yer legs can never stand it, nor yet yer stomach. Stands to reason, even if you can't stand nor got no reason.'

'Oh shut yer mouth an' give yer arse a chance,' said Godwin. Nasty lot they Godwins when they'd had a drop to drink. Runs in the fambly, nastyness in the blood, low bred uns; in goes the drink an' out comes the nastiness. I turned my back on him. 'Have a drink, Percy,' I says. Alf went on playin' for all he was worth an' we kept on singin', those of us as could. Colonel, fr'instance was more like croakin', still the old feller was doin' the best he could, not everybody got a good voice like me an' Percy. Mind it were a good night, we had a rare old time.

'What about another drink, George?' asked Alf.

'I've bought you two an' I aint buyin' you no more,' I said.

'Time I stopped playin' then,' he said.

'Don't stop playin',' shouted Godwin, 'I be only just gettin' into me stride.'

'Buy 'im a drink then,' I said.

'Bring 'im a drink,' Godwin shouted to Percy, 'I don't mind buyin' the pianner player a drink even if others do begrudge 'im.'

Oh, that's the way it is, I thought to meself. Well, bagger the baggers, the beer, the barrer an' the pianner, let 'em 'ave a barney for all I care, I thought to meself.

'Knocked 'em in the Old Kent Road' we sang. Ah, there was some there as I'd a liked to have knocked down the Old Kent Road or into Noakes's pond. That would have made some on 'em splutter. Damn my rags if it 'ouldn't. Begrudge a man a drink indeed, I've never been the sort to begrudge a man a drink, but that don't mean I'd encourage a man to make a pig of hisself. Neither more do I hold with always havin' me hand in me pocket. Old Godwin had no cause to say a thing like that, not to me. Not after I saved him from a hiding – Percy would have made mincemeat of the old fool. And as fer tellin' me to shut me mouth and the rest on't, that were uncalled for, but it just showed what a vulgar, low bred sort o' feller he was when the drink got talkin'.

Where did you get that hat?
Where did you get that tile?
Isn't it a nobby one, and just the proper style?'

There, I've still gotta fairish voice; but, Rajah, rhubarb, didn't I let meself go on that un that night when old Tom swallered his barrer.

What? What? . . . Oh, I'm comin' to that, all in good time, if you'd only let me. You'm a good boy, but you will keep interruptin', it's a reg'lar 'abit you've got. You want to get out of it else you'll never learn anythin'. I'm allus sayin' to old Colonel, 'Don't interrupt when I'm talkin'. I can do all what's needed o' that, your job's listenin'.' Anyway old Colonel's a proper haggler, he've no idea how to tell a tale, kip beatin' about the bush instead o' gettin' on with it.

'D'ye ken John Peel'. We didn't half let go on that un I remember. There's nothing like a good old rousin' song to cheer you up. But they got to be sung right, not like old Sam do sing 'em at the concerts, that ain't no bottle, but then he ain't no bottle neither, I don't know how our Aggie do put up with him.

Old Tom weren't half roarin' away that night, how he was goin' to get wum God only knew, Tom he were past knowin' or carin'. Well, I stopped on for a bit an' then I said goodnight to 'em all. 'Goodnight, Tom,' I said, 'an' mind how you do go if you can go at all.'

'Goo,' he answered, 'I'll goo when I'm ready an' not afore.'

'Go when you please, 'tis a wonder where you put all that beer, you must be right full up, it'll be sloppin' out of you, the amount you've had.' I told him.

'Ah,' he said, 'I've had a drop.'

'How be you gwaine to get wum?' I asked'n.

'I got me barrer, I'll hold tight to me barrer, but I ain't gwaine yet awhile. I be goin' to sing "Boiled Beef an' Carrots" now,' he said.

'Well, goodnight to you, Tom, ole feller.' I spoke civil to'n despite everything, let bygones be bygones, I allus say. And then I left. Why I left then I can't rightly remember, 'tis so long ago, I con't remember everything but 'tis no matter now. And that were that, or so I thought at the time. But next day 'twere the talk of the place, Tom Godwin had bin an' swallered his barrer. Ever afterwards he were known as the man who swallered a wheelbarrow.

* * * * *

Uncle George paused, filled his pipe and told me to fetch some more cider; saying, 'Telling that story have given me a real swaller too.'

When I returned with the cider Uncle was gazing pensively at his beloved wheelbarrow. I filled the mug and Uncle swallowed the cider in a manner which would not have disgraced Tom Godwin himself.

'That ain't quite the end of the story, mind,' he said. 'I heard more from Percy Ludgater. Seemingly Tom hadn't bin payin' for the beer as he had it. Apparently he'd bin in earlier an' had one drink an' when he paid for that 'un he'd pulled out a fistful of money, notes an' all. So Percy thought there was no need to worrit on that account. Old Tom were the last to leave an' just as he were gwaine Percy caught hold of his arm an' said "What about settlin' up for the beer, Tom?" That were a bit of a shock to Tom. "It comes to a pretty old penny," Percy said. "That's all right," says Tom, fumblin' in his pockets, "I got plenty." But he didn't find it in the fust pocket, nor the next, not unless you call one and druppence ha'penny plenty. So he tried another pocket, then another, he turned all his pockets out, produced string, a knife, ole broken bootlaces an' a deal of rubbish but no money.

'"'Tis a damn funny thing," says Tom, lookin' puzzled, "but I had plenty o' money when I set out, must 'ave lost it or bin robbed – better fetch the bobby, Percy." Percy didn't want no truck with the bobby, I'll warrant. Then Old Tom remembered. "I paid the money to Edgar for the barrer. I'll pay you another day, Percy." That weren't no good to Percy, but Percy were a cunnin' old varmint. "I'm sorry, Tom, but if you wunt pay I'll have to call the bobby. I shan't like doin' it but a man gotta look after hisself."

'Old Tom were dead against the bobby bein' called, although he'd bin keen enough on the idea when 'twas his idea.

'"Tell you what, Tom," says Percy, "we don't want no trouble."

'"No, we don't want no trouble," agrees Tom.

'"You let me have yer barrer and we be all square. No debts, no bobby, no trouble, all fair an' square, good friends an' no more said."

'"I do want me barrer, thee cosn't 'ave me barrer," says Tom.

'"I do want my money, an' if I can't have it I do want thy barrer. Why, 'tis legally mine, I do know the law, gotta know the law in my business. Bobby'll tell 'e that when he do come."

'"He ain't comin'," said Tom. "You said he ain't."

'"No more he ain't if you agree to let me have thy barrer," says Percy.

'Well, the long and the short of it were, poor old Tom pleaded an' pleaded and Percy kept on threatenin' until Tom agreed to part with his barrer. Then overcome by the beer an' all on't the poor old fella fell to the ground an' Percy put'n in a shed for the night.

'Next mornin' Percy was wakened by a hammerin' an' a yammerin'. Lookin' out of the window he sees old Tom. "Somebody's stole me barrer" he were a yellin'. "Get the bobby, get the bobby. I'll get the bobby." Seemingly Percy had took the barrer away somewhere where old Tom couldn't get at'n. Locked and barred it up I'll warrant.

'"Theest got no barrer for anybody to steal," Percy yelled at 'im, "and if you don't shut up and git off from here I'll get the bobby."

'Well, to cut a long story short, that were that. Tom lost his barrer and thic Percy stuck to'n. Tom went to see him again later, but Percy wouldn't part. "A deal's a deal," Percy told him. "And you gotta stick to't, that's the law, an' I'm stickin' to the barrer." Broke poor old Tom's heart I reckon. He never came down to the village no more after that. Old Percy put the tale round about swallerin' the barrer, but it didn't do Percy any good in the long run, folk didn't think much of him after that. An' what's more, he never had no use out of the barrer neither, 'cos he broke his leg soon after and could never walk again without two sticks. An' a man who got two sticks in his hands got no hands left to trundle a barrer. Serve'n right too.

'I reckon the business finished old Edgar off too, he were right upset about it and even promised to make old Tom another barrer. But he died afore he could do it, reckon it was that business what done it, him bein' old an' ill an' all. No, poor old Edgar never made another barrer.'

'But what about your barrow, Uncle?'

'What barrow?'

'That barrow there, Uncle, your barrow. You said that was the last barrow Mr Bailey made.'

'So 'twas, soak me bob if it ain't.'

'But Mr Godwin's was the last.'

'So it were.'

'But . . .'

''Tis the same barrer, me boy.'

'But Percy Ludgater had that one.'

'So he did, locked up in his shed and no use to'n at all, but he wouldn't part with him.'

'How . . .'

'Well, time went by. Percy had broken his legs, ole Edgar had died, then old Tom, he went an' died an' folk remembered about the barrer business an' talked about it. By an' by, Percy began to fade.'

'And . . .'

'I went to see Percy. "Percy," I said, "that business about the barrer's playin' on yer mind, you'll get no peace 'til you've parted with'n."

'"You think so, George?" said Percy.

'"I reckon so, Percy," I said, "I've bin thinkin' a lot about it."

'"There might be summat in what you say, George," he said, "I'll think about it."

'"Ah," I told'n, "You think about it, Percy, an' you'll come to realise I'm right, you'll get no peace o' mind 'til you've parted with that barrer." An' I were right, old Percy got no peace 'til he parted with that barrer. I saw to that.'

We gazed, Uncle and I, at the wheelbarrow.

'Rajah rhubarb!' exclaimed Uncle, 'that's a toppin' barrer, the last and the finest Edgar ever made.'

Chapter Three

The Pursuit of Uncle George

'Our George don't seem a right un,' said Father.

'I've known that for a long time,' said Mother. 'He's far from being a right one, perhaps if he'd got married he would have improved. But as it is, all on his own with no one to look after him, no one to make him keep himself up together, he goes from bad to worse. I've often thought he might have been better if he'd had a good wife round him – and not only that, he wouldn't have been down here every whipstitch, tormenting me, causing trouble and eating me out of house and home. But who would have married him, the cratur, no decent, self-respecting woman would ever have looked at him.'

'Our George were a smart chap when he was young,' said Father. 'I can't understand why you don't like him and why you're always so nasty gritted about him. I dare say there's many a woman what would have been only too pleased to have him for a husband, but our George never took any interest in women.'

'I expect there's a good many women who look at him and thank heaven that they are not wedded to him.'

'Our George don't seem himself,' said Father.

'Oh!' said Mother. 'If he isn't himself, who is he?'

'That's what I can't fathom, I wish I could.'

'I wish he was somebody else and somewhere else. Many's the time I wished he was in Jericho.'

'I said to him only the other day, "George," I said, "are you all right?"'

'I must admit, he does seem a bit strange. Strange for him, I mean, he's always been . . .'

'So you've noticed it, Ethel, old lady,' said Father.

I wasn't very old at the time but I too, had noticed something strange about Uncle George. He seemed to have lost his usual bonhomie, bluster and bounce; worse, he

appeared to have a rather furtive manner. He kept looking
over his shoulder, was unnaturally quiet and subdued at
times. Coming home from school, I'd seen him slinking out
of his shop and scuttling along the street. While in his
garden, he stopped whatever he was doing every now and
then and looked about and listened as if he was expecting
somebody. And when Micah looked over the hedge he was
not greeted with shouts of abuse. Twice I found him in the
garden shed in such a way to suggest that he was hiding.
He'd also altered his times and routes in and around the
village.

'I don't like it and that's a fact,' said Father, putting his
newspaper aside. 'I'm off to see Aggie to see what she do
think about it.'

On the way to Aunt Aggie's we saw a man wearing a
battered trilby hat, ragged jacket and baggy trousers coming
towards us.

'Here's old Colonel,' said Father, 'we'll stop and have a
word with him, he might know summat we don't know about
our George. Him, and our George are pretty thick, your
Uncle may have confided in him. It might be he's ailing and
don't like to tell the fambly – our George never did like
worrying the fambly. I might pop along to see Dr Higgins,
he might know summat. Good God Almighty, I hope it ain't
a Royal Infirmary job. . . Here's Colonel. . . Evening, Colonel, how are you?'

'Fair to middlin', fair to middlin', could be better, could
be wuss. Mustn't grumble, a lot wuss than me.'

'Worse than you, Colonel?'

'Ah, right wusser, I'd aim.'

'Oh dear.'

'Never mind, kip smilin', I allus say.'

'Seen our George?'

'No, not lately. Funny you should mention it but he do
seem to have started kippin' hisself to hisself like.'

'Is he all right, do you think?'

'Oh, ah, him's all right, he do drink an' smoke an' cuss an'
all.'

'You don't think he's ill then, he hasn't said anything to
you?'

'He've said a lot to me, but he haven't said anything about
bein' bad, 'cept his usual complaints which he do allus seem

to enjoy. Still, it's funny you should ask that 'cos he have bin asking me some funny things.'

'Such as?'

'Well, lately he have bin asking me to goo on the bread round with him, kip on sayin', "Come on the round with me, Colonel." Now he knows I can't do that, I be helpin' Noakes with his hay, but he do still kip askin'. "Try an' come, Colonel," he do say. He bin askin' Reuben the same. 'Tis funny as he do seem to crave company and yet kip hisself to hisself.'

Father bid Colonel goodnight and we hurried on towards Aunt Aggie's house. 'I don't like the sounds of it,' said Father as we waited for Aunt Aggie to open the door.

'Sam's poorly,' she said as soon as she saw us. 'The poor old fella isn't himself.' The way she said it and the way she was dressed could have led those who did not know her to suppose that she had just returned from his funeral. 'Not himself at all,' she said as she led us into the living room.

'Seems as no-one's himself round here,' muttered Father. 'Our George ain't himself, even Colonel ain't hisself, working reg'lar, that ain't like him.'

We entered the living room. Uncle Sam was slumped in an easy chair, looking morose, in fact looking very much his usual self.

'No change there,' whispered Father.

Aunt Aggie had rushed over to her husband. 'Let me put you comfy,' she said, pulling a cushion from behind his back, plumping it and then putting it gently behind him again. Turning and facing us, she said, 'There, you can see he's not himself, poor old fella.' Then addressing herself directly to the poor old fella, 'Feeling any better after the pills?'

'Aargh, aargh,' grunted Uncle Sam.

'The doctor said they'd take a little time to work. Are they working, do you think?'

'Aargh, aargh,' grunted Sam, 'I can feel 'em working.'

'It's his head again and his back and his poor old tummy,' explained Aggie, 'It plays him up. I've told him he goes at it too hard. Steady up, old fella, I say to him, or your head will be at it again.'

Uncle Sam had not acknowledged our presence yet, so Father spoke to him. 'Been a nice day, Sam.'

'An't noticed it.' said Sam.

'They've come to see you, Sam,' said Aunt Aggie. 'Isn't that nice of them?'

Getting no response Aunt Aggie turned to us and said, 'He's a bit downy, he'll brighten up in a minute.'

'I could do with another cup of tea and another of those dripping cakes,' said Sam.

'There, there, you see he's getting quite chirpy already!' exclaimed Aunt Aggie.

Sam tugged at his large, drooping moustache and turned his red-rimmed eyes towards us. 'Come to see me, have you?'

'Really I came to see Aggie about our George,' said Father.

'They ain't come to see me, Aggie,' complained Uncle Sam. 'I thought it weren't likely, no one comes to see me unless they want summat.'

'It's about our George . . .' began Father.

'I think I could manage another dripping cake,' said Sam.

After Aunt Aggie had ministered to Sam, which included handing him two more dripping cakes, another cup of tea, re-arranging his cushions, feeling his forehead and wiping his chin – he was as Father often observed, a disgusting eater – she said, 'What did you say about George?'

'He don't seem a right un, he ain't hisself, seems as if he've got something on his mind,' Father said.

'I have wondered if there's something worrying him,' replied Aunt Aggie. 'He keeps coming here. Of course, we're glad to see him. We're glad to see him, aren't we, Sam? But it's not like him to always be here and at such peculiar times. Peculiar, I said, didn't I, Sam? Twice I've been down to his house in the evening and both times he hasn't answered the door although I knew he was there – he's taken to bolting the door you know. Once I saw him peeping out between the curtains of his bedroom and when I shouted he came down and said, "Oh, it's you, Aggie." Ever so pleased he was when he knew it was me. When I said to him, just in fun mind, "Who are you hiding from?" he gave me such an old fashioned look. Oh, I know I shouldn't, but I couldn't help laughing. You remember, Sam, I said to you that George was hiding.'

'I remember,' said Sam, brightening himself and taking off his hat.

'There, there, you'll feel better without that nasty old hat on your head. Can't understand why you keep it on so much,' said Aggie. 'He will keep it on. I've told him his head would be better without it, but he's so strong willed you know.'

'It's my opinion,' said Sam, 'that he's been up to something and the law's after him. He've got a shifty look. I allus knowed they'd be after him sooner or later.'

'Now, now, Sam, you mustn't say that about George,' admonished Aunt Aggie.

'You ask my opinion and when I give it that ain't right,' said Sam, who belched as if to signal his disapproval of the world in general.

'Nasty old wind, you'll be better now you've got rid of it, old fella. Would you like a ciggie now?'

Aunt Aggie gave him a cigarette and struck a match for him. He did not thank her, he never thanked her for any of the many services she did for him, neither did she expect it. Just to fuss over him, and fuss she did, was reward enough.

'On the other hand,' said Sam, 'he might have the moneylenders after him.'

'Not our George, he ain't short of a penny,' said Father.

'They'll hound a man,' said Sam.

'He've been asking Colonel and Reuben to go on the round with him.'

'P'rhaps he've been carrying on with a married 'oman and her husband's atter him,' said Uncle Sam, showing some excitement.

'Not our George, he've never had any interest in women!' exclaimed Father.

'You can never tell, not where women's concerned,' said Uncle Sam.

'Oh dear, I hope we're not going to have a scandal in the family,' cried Aunt Aggie.

'Or,' said Sam, 'could be he's thinkin' about doin' himself in. Some do you know, this is a famous district for suicides. Why, I remember . . .'

'Now, now, Sam,' whispered Aunt Aggie.

Sam relapsed into sullen silence. Father said he thought he would have a cup of tea after all.

'I'll make a fresh pot, it'll cheer us all up,' said Aunt Aggie.

She scuttled out of the room while the three of us sat there in a silence only broken by the breaking of wind by Uncle Sam.

'There, there,' said Aunt Aggie on her return, 'a nice pot of tea and some biscuits, now we'll be all right.'

'Of course, he's all alone down there, poor old devil, I expect he . . .' began Father.

'I'll have a word with the vicar, that's what I'll do. He's always such a comfort in times like this,' said Aunt Aggie, pouring tea. 'Like another ciggie, Sam? Oh, the poor old fella, just look at him.'

Sam looked more mournful than when we'd arrived, gaunt and dismal with shoulders hunched.

'Don't upset yourself, old fella,' said Aunt Aggie, patting the old fella's knee.

'I'm just wondering how he'll do it,' muttered Sam. 'Hanging would be the best job for him I should think. With his weight he'd fall well.'

'I don't hold with that sort of talk,' declared Father. 'You're upsetting the boy here, and me and Aggie.'

'George was always so full of life,' said Aunt Aggie, 'To think it's come to this. Oh, dear oh!'

'It haven't come to that,' expostulated Father.

'It might,' said Sam. 'Moneylenders will hound a man. I remember when Jack Perkins got into their hands and all them men with big black hats were atter him . . .'

'Our George is all right for money . . .'

'And I remember when Davis were caught wi' a married woman. That were a nasty business, blood and bruises an' broken bones . . .'

'I'll have a word with the vicar.'

'Ethel don't like the sound on't. No more do Colonel.'

''Tis a good job 'tis summer time,' said Uncle Sam, 'I do hate funerals in the winter, you get so cold hangin' about round the grave.'

'Now look here,' said Father, a touch of asperity in his voice, 'we don't want that sort of talk.' Father rose to his feet and said 'I'm going home.'

Aunt Aggie followed us down the passage saying 'You mustn't take any notice of Sam, the poor old fella's tired.'

'Tired, be damned,' snorted Father, 'he were born tired.'

'Now, now,' pleaded Aunt Aggie, 'we're all upset and we're saying things we shouldn't. George isn't himself. Sam isn't himself, none of us are ourselves, I shan't sleep a wink tonight.'

As she closed the door she whispered, 'I'll see what the vicar has to say.'

Father walked briskly along the street, I almost had to run to keep up with him. 'A complete waste of time that was,' he said angrily.

'Poor Uncle George,' I said, biting my lip.

'Don't you worry, boy,' said Father gently. 'He'll be all right, as he says you can't keep a good man down.'

'What about Uncle Sam, what's the matter with him? Is he very ill? Is he going to die instead?'

'There's nothing the matter with him, except idleness and greed. And your aunt's that soft about him, keep fussing and cosseting him, it turns my stomach over to see her at it. The chap's no bottle, no bottle at all.'

★ ★ ★ ★ ★

The summer term ended and I was able to accompany Uncle George on his bread round. Uncle seemed comparatively cheerful as we set off with the horse and baker's van. 'Thic bread,' said Uncle, 'smells especially good today, I hope the baggers do appreciate it, but nothing 'ould please some on 'em. Some on 'em grumble an' grouse an' complain about everything. . .'

I was only half listening to him as we clip-clopped along the road on that fine fresh summer's morning, my mind and my eyes were concerned with other things. Any minute, as we drew further from the village, I expected men with large black hats to appear, or an irate husband – perhaps several irate husbands – blackguards, blackmailers, gangsters, cut-throats, or plain-clothed detectives. Father had mentioned black-guards, Uncle Sam had mentioned blackmailers, – I had no idea what blackguards or blackmailers looked like, presumably they would be dressed in black, possibly with tall black hats, perhaps hardly distinguishable from the moneylenders with their black hats. The gangsters, cut-throats and detectives were my own ideas; gangsters, I knew, also wore big hats, cut-throats would be wearing caps pulled well down, detectives would be hawk-eyed; all this I knew from reading about Sexton Blake.

But everything seemed peaceful, not a big black hat in sight, no sign of anyone who looked remotely like a desperado.

Husbands we saw in field and farm, but they all seemed placid enough and most of them hailed us in a friendly fashion.

'What's the matter, boy?' asked Uncle George. 'Lost your tongue?'

He handed me the reins and started filling his pipe. Out of the corner of my eye I watched him. How steady his hands were, he even started whistling. How could he be so calm I wondered when any moment black-hatted men or irate husbands may be lurking round the next corner waiting to pounce on him.

We delivered bread to customers. Uncle gossiped as usual with the women, where there were men present he gave advice on gardening and other subjects, accepted a cup of tea here, sampled a glass of cider or home-made wine there, exchanged pleasantries with men we met on the road. We were halfway round without any of the incidents I had pictured in my mind occuring.

There were incidents, it would be impossible to spend a couple of hours in Uncle George's company without some incident. Mrs Jones, who lived in the thatched house, complained about last week's bread; 'It was black, burnt to a cinder.'

'Lar, bless you, Missus,' rumbled Uncle George, 'that were crusty bread, special crusty bread.'

'It was black, the crust was burnt to a cinder.'

'Charcoal, Missus, good for the digestion, lucky to get such fine, well-cooked, crusty bread. Different from that half baked stuff some have got to have from bakers what don't know their job.'

'Well, I don't want any more of that kind of stuff. It isn't fit for a dog.'

'Dogs do love it, Missus, they do go mad about it, trouble is dogs don't often get the chance on't.'

'My dog wouldn't look at it.'

'And I wouldn't look at your dog. A nasty, pampered, unhealthy, ill natured cratur he is. He ain't fit to look at my bread. If I'd known as you was givin' him my bread I 'ouldn't 'ave let you have any. If you wants pappy bread for you an' your pappy dog, go to a pappy baker for't.'

'That's a fine way to talk to a customer.'

'You're one to talk, Missus, insultin' me an' my beautiful bread. You've cut me to the quick an' I've no more to say to you.'

'I'll get my bread in future from a baker with a civil tongue in his head.'

'What's the good of her talkin',' said Uncle George when we were back in the van. 'There ain't no other baker for miles. I'll put aside some part-cooked bread, that'll teach her, she'll soon be crying out for some well-baked stuff, I'll warrant. But I think I'll give her a miss the next time round, let her feel the want of bread.'

We stopped almost an hour with Mr and Mrs Day. All went merrily, there was cider for Uncle, lemonade for me, home-made cakes for both of us. Uncle discoursed about the latest murder, going into detail, occasionally muttering 'There's some damned bad baggers about, damn my rags if there ain't.' Then we went to see Mr Day's pigs. 'What d'you think of them, George?' he asked.

'They do need some pig powders,' said Uncle.

'Whatever for?' asked Mr Day.

'Put some bloom on 'em.'

'Bloom? Bloom? They got bloom, as fine a bunch of pigs as you'd see.'

'You ain't seen mine, or you'd never say that,' said Uncle George.

'Perhaps you don't know as much about pigs as you think you do,' replied Mr. Day. We walked back to the house in silence.

'Another mug of cider, or a cup of tea before you go?' asked Mrs Day cheerfully from the doorway.

'He don't want no more cider, nor yet tea,' said Mr Day.

'Oh, all right,' said Mrs Day, going back inside the house.

Uncle took his basket off the garden wall, took a few paces down the path, stopped and turned to face Mr Day, 'No, I don't want no more of your cider, Jack, I can't take much of that ole ropey stuff.'

'Ho! Me cider's ropey now, you liked it well enough just now.'

'I'll take a tot or two outa politeness, but there's a limit even to politeness, a man can't be expected to punish hisself unmercifully just on account of politeness.'

'Seems to me, George, as you ain't no better a judge of cider than you be of pigs.'

'Your garden ain't doin' very well this year, Jack,' said Uncle, scowling at some cabbages. 'I got some master uns at my place. Seems as it ain't goin' too good with you this year. Look at them apples, poor little scabby things. No, you ain't makin' much of a go on't this year, perhaps you'll do better next year if I give you a bit of advice at the right time – providin' you got the sense to take heed.'

'It's time you were off, George.'

Mrs Day's head appeared from the window. 'I've got the kettle on, sure you won't stop for a cup?' she shouted.

'Not today thank you, I've stopped here long enough,' replied Uncle and then walked quickly down the path. 'That sour old cider do make Jack Day rasty,' Uncle said, 'An' tis no wonder, it's like puttin' vinegar in your belly.'

We were approaching the crossroads and standing by the signpost was a woman. As we neared the crossroads she stepped forward, almost in the path of the horse. Uncle George drew the reins in.

'Hello, George,' said the woman, 'I thought you were never coming.'

And then, to my surprise, she climbed into the van and sat down on the seat beside me.

'Who's this?' she asked Uncle.

'He's my nephew.'

'Your brother's boy? I haven't met your family yet.'

'No,' said Uncle George, who, I thought, was looking rather peculiar. 'No, you ain't.'

She was middle-aged, rather smartly dressed and highly scented. 'Aren't you going to introduce me?' she asked Uncle.

'This is Mrs Aspall,' said Uncle.

We stopped at a cottage. 'Three loaves here,' muttered Uncle.

'Your nephew will take them, I'm sure,' the woman said quickly.

'Oh ah, oh ah,' murmured Uncle George uncomfortably.

'There's a good little man,' she said as I set off to the cottage.

When I returned, she had moved along the seat towards Uncle and I had to sit on the other side of her. There was not a lot of room on the seat for three of us, nevertheless as we drove along I couldn't help thinking that she was sitting unnecesssarily close to Uncle George. She did not talk a lot and what she did say did not seem of much consequence. Uncle barely spoke at all and when he did it was in monosyllables but he seemed to be ill at ease and kept rubbing his finger around the inside of the red spotted handkerchief he used as a neckerchief. Occasionally he mopped his face or blew his nose in another spotted handkerchief. Uncle George was quite definitely not himself. For two miles she rode with us. When we stopped to deliver bread at several houses she sat in the van alone, powdering her nose and cheeks and looking in a little glass. When we stopped at a solitary house she said, 'There's a good little man, run along and deliver the bread for your Uncle.' And while I delivered the bread she sat just as close to him, and, I fancy, had a great deal more to say than when I was in the van.

I took a dislike to her. I did not like the look on her face, I didn't like the smell of her scent, I did not like her calling me 'little man' or ordering me to deliver the bread. I hated that little glass of hers that glinted in the sunlight, but most of all I hated the way she kept nudging closer and closer to Uncle George, and the way it embarassed him.

At first I had thought she was only an acquaintance of Uncle George's to whom he was giving a lift. Gradually it dawned upon me; Uncle Sam was right after all, Uncle George was carrying on with a married woman. What puzzled me most was, of all the dozens of married women Uncle George knew, why did he have to choose this particular one.

I remembered other things Uncle Sam had said; blood and bruises and broken bones. Should I tell Father, or perhaps Aunt Aggie, or should I keep this guilty secret of Uncle George's. Or again, it might be better to confide in Colonel or Reuben. But she did not seem the sort of woman to run the risk of blood and bruises and broken bones over. It was all very puzzling and Uncle George didn't seem a bit happy about it.

More thoughts crowded my mind – I was half regretting we hadn't been set upon by big black-hatted men. I tried to obtain some comfort by remembering Father's words, 'Our George isn't interested in women.' And, to be sure, he hadn't the appearance of a man particularly interested in her. Perhaps it was only a chance encounter, perhaps I was only imagining that there was more to it than that. Dear God, make it only my imagination, if Uncle George wants to carry on with women, married or unmarried, send this one away and bring him a different one.

But my hopes were dashed when she stepped out of the van. 'Goodbye, George,' she said, 'I'll see you next week.'

We drove on, Uncle looked glum, I felt glum, we scarcely spoke to each other. The sun shone but the world seemed dark.

As we were unharnessing the horse, Uncle George very quietly said, 'I'd take it as a favour, boy, if you kept mum about our passenger today.'

* * * * *

During the following week, there she was waiting for Uncle George on another of his rounds, and another, and another. On the third time of that week, she opened her handbag and gave me a bag of sweets. The first sweet tasted of scent and I swallowed it as quickly as possible; the second tasted of scent, I spat it out when she wasn't looking and did not try another. As Uncle George had said; a man can't be expected to punish his stomach unmercifully just on account of politeness.

When Uncle George came to lunch on the Sunday, he ate with his usual enjoyment, but did not seem to have much appetite for some of the topics which usually occupied his and Father's Sunday afternoons. He had little enthusiasm for local gossip or the crop of scandals in *The News of the World*. Not altogether surprising in one who would almost certainly be the subject of gossip and scandal sooner or later. But Father of course did not know this and was genuinely puzzled. In an effort to cheer Uncle, Father said, 'Do Mrs Peabody still go up to the spinney to meet her fancy chap, do you know, George?'

Uncle merely grunted. I felt sorry for him. Father had unwittingly asked a most embarassing question, Uncle himself was probably going to some spinney to meet Mrs Aspall – and I suddenly realised with some shock that Uncle was 'a fancy man.'

'Our George ain't himself, Ethel,' whispered Father when Uncle was having a nap.

'No, he isn't,' replied Mother, 'and he's a sight better when he isn't himself. If only he'd steady down on eating and drinking he'd be almost bearable. Whoever he is he's still eating me out of house and home.'

'That's a good sign, that is,' said Father, looking relieved. 'If he can still eat well it can't be his health. But I still think I'll have another word with our Aggie – see if she knows anything. I'd have gone before, but that old Sam takes some sticking.'

Later that afternoon, while I was in the street, talking to Colonel, I saw Mrs Aspall walking quickly in the direction of Uncle George's house. 'Oho!' exclaimed Colonel, 'thur's that Mrs Aspall, wonder what brings her down here? What's her atter I should like to know?'

I could have said Uncle George, but instead I asked if he knew her. 'In a manner o' speaking. Her's a widder 'oman, in fact 'er's a widder twice over, her've buried two and I'd aim as hers lookin' fer another.'

On Tuesday evening I went down to see Uncle George and to my surprise and consternation found Mrs Aspall in the garden with him. My loyalty to Uncle George was strained to breaking point, especially when Father asked me what Uncle had been doing in the garden that evening. But by next day it was all over the village – 'Old George has got a woman.'

By the end of the week all caution had been thrown to the wind, she was in the shop and they were seen openly walking side by side in the village.

'Come on, boy,' said Father one Saturday evening, 'let's go and see what your Aunt Aggie has got to say about this how-d'ye-do.'

'Oh, come on in quickly,' whispered Aunt Aggie. 'Don't let people see us talking out here. Oh, I've scarce dared to go out this last few days. Everybody's talking and asking questions.'

Uncle Sam was in his usual chair and looking almost cheerful. 'You've come then,' he said.

'The old fella's been quite bright this last few days,' said Aunt Aggie, 'which is such a blessing with what's going on. Yes, yes, he's rallied and he's been such a tower of strength, bless the old fella's heart.'

'Seems as there's something in it by all accounts,' said Father. 'But our George ain't said a word to me.'

'I don't like it, I don't like it,' said Aunt Aggie. 'A few days ago he came here and he looked so hang-dog, I said to him, I did, I said to him – of course I didn't know then what I know now – but I said to him, "George," I said, "if there's anything worrying you, why don't you have a word with the vicar?" And he said, "Vicar will know soon enough." Now that was a funny thing to say . . .'

'I knowed it, I knowed it,' said Sam. 'What did I say to you t'other day? There's a 'oman in it, that's what I said.'

'You did, old fella, you've got a brain in that poor old head of yours,' said Aunt Aggie.

'And it an't even started yet, or if it have we don't know all on't yet,' said Sam.

'Why? What else, Sam, what else?' cried Aunt Aggie.

'For all we know there might be more women, when a man of George's age do start on this caper there's no stoppin' 'em and when one ain't enough a dozen ain't too many.'

'Not our George,' said Father.

'Ah, that's what you said afore,' said Sam craftily, 'an' you was wrong. Probably bin goin' on for years, him a baker an' all an' calling on women while their 'usbands be away.'

'Oh, Sam, old fella don't say that.'

'I do say it an' I do say more. It wun't end just at that. What did I tell ye t'other day? Thur's the moneylenders to follow . . .'

'Our George is all right for money,' said Father.

'You said t'other day as he weren't int'rested in women, but now you knows different,' said Sam.

'But what's our George havin' been seen with this woman got to do with moneylenders?' demanded Father.

'One 'oman you thinks now,' replied Uncle Sam, 'but in a wik or two it might be a sight more'n one. An' we don't know what it's costin' him, jools an' suchlike – an' that's where the moneylenders come in.'

I had never known Uncle Sam so talkative, Aunt Aggie so flabbergasted – and as for Father, he did not seem to have made up his mind whether to be angry, incredulous or just worried.

'Then, as I said t'other day, suicide,' said Sam.

'I've heard enough of this nonsense,' said Father.

'Ah, you called it nonsense t'other day, but as you know now it weren't all nonsense an' time'll tell whether rest on't weren't nonsense, you mark my words,' said Uncle Sam. All the excitement must have exhausted him, because at this point the old fella suddenly closed his eyes and went to sleep and was soon snoring loudly.

'Lord, bless me soul, Aggie,' exclaimed Father. 'How do you ever sleep with that sort of racket at nights. Forty steam engines would have a job to beat it.'

'It's all those brains he's got in his poor old head what does it, I expect,' said Aunt Aggie proudly.

'It don't sound right, whatever's the cause on't.'

'Beat to the world, bathered right out, bless him,' said Aunt Aggie gazing fondly at her slumbering husband.

'I can't sleep, not to say proper, I keep wakin' up at nights thinking about this business over our George,' said Father. 'It's the talk of the place, it ain't like him, I can't understand what makes him do it, he've never had no time for women.'

'That's just the trouble,' said Aunt Aggie, 'He isn't doing anything. It's her, that Mrs Asp. She's chasing our brother George – and he don't know what to do.'

Uncle Sam roused himself just as we were leaving, to say somewhat sleepily, 'Kids, I wonder how many kids he've got about the district?'

Out in the street Father said, 'I don't like that Sam Fisher, I only keep a civil tongue in my head for the sake of your aunt.'

We met Colonel; 'I'm just goin' down to the Lion. We don't see George in there much of an evenin'. Still, I expect he's too busy dippin' his wick to have time to wet his whistle o' nights.' Father merely grunted.

'I don't know what to make on't,' said Father when we were back home. 'I can't understand what have come over our George. That Sam's filling our Aggie's head with a lot of wicked rubbish. Our Aggie says George is being chased, but I can't believe a man like George, not with his abilities, would suffer that. Why, he's got a head on him like a lawyer.'

'More like a turnip,' said Mother. 'And you know the saying, there's no fool like an old fool.'

'It's not like our George, he've always been able to handle people and many's the scrape he's got hisself out of.'

'All bluster he is, he's foxed, that's what he is; that, or he's besotted with her.'

'I just don't know what to think, Ethel, old lady. I've got to the state when I don't know what'll happen next.'

We hadn't long to wait to know what would happen next. After lunch on Sunday, just when Father and Uncle George had had a cup of tea and were preparing – as Uncle said – 'for forty winks', there was a sharp rat-tat-tat on the door.

'Who can that be at this hour of the day,' grumbled Father, annoyed at being disturbed, 'Go and see who it is, Ethel.'

Mother returned looking woebegone. 'It's someone to see George – is he asleep? Oh, it's that woman, Mrs Aspall, what shall I do, shall I ask her in?'

Mother's problem was more or less solved by Mrs Aspall's calling, 'Shall I come on in?' And without waiting for an answer, in she came.

'Hello, hello, hello,' she said; all got up, as Mother said afterwards, fit to kill. 'So you're George's brother, you're his sister-in-law, so nice to meet you at last. And the little man, we've met before, we're old friends. I'm Mrs Aspall, Mrs A for short, but not for long, perhaps. But you two must call me Mavis and the little man can call me Aunty. Oh, look at George, fast asleep, doesn't he look funny when he's bye-byes. Come on, George, my lad, wake up.'

Uncle George woke up with a start and when he saw Mrs Aspall he looked startled. 'Come along, George,' she said gaily, a shade too gaily.

Uncle George went, as Mother later remarked, 'like a lamb to the slaughter.'

'Oh, dear oh,' said Father when they had gone.

'That woman is going to marry George,' announced Mother. 'Aggie was right, she was chasing him and I think she's caught him.'

'She ain't the right sort for our George,' said Father, holding his head in his hands.

'I can't see what our George do see in her,' said Father some time later. 'What does he want with a woman like that?'

'He doesn't want her, that's obvious. It's as plain as a pike staff,' answered Mother. 'And if you weren't so soft, you'd see it, and if that great George wasn't so soft he wouldn't have allowed it to go so far as it has. The great, fat, sawny cratur, he'll be wed to her before he knows where he is.'

*   *   *   *   *

After Mrs Aspall's visit to us; having broken the ice, as it were, with the family, the pursuit of Uncle George gathered strength. Mrs Aspall was continually seen in Uncle's company. In the evenings she was in the garden with him or helping him with his livestock. During the day she rode boldly beside him through the village in the baker's van. Or in the shop, leaning on the counter, talking to him, even showing resentment at the arrival of a customer. Soon she was on the other side of the counter, serving the customers.

'And there he is, the great soft,' said Mother, 'just allowing himself to get deeper and deeper into the trap.'

'I can't understand him, it ain't like him, he don't seem to be himself. I'll have to speak to him. . .'

'You!' snorted Mother, 'you've had chance enough, you'll never say a word, you never do. And as for him – if he's that soft – huh! He's never been backward with interfering in other people's business, it's a pity he doesn't interfere in his own. I must admit I can't understand him – but then I never could.'

'She's asked me to decorate the shop,' said Uncle Sam, 'But Aggie says I'm not to do it.'

'When I went down to tidy George up,' said a very irate Aunt Aggie, a few days later, 'that woman had been there, moving everything about, poking and prying. "Who's been doing this?" I asked George. "She've done it," he said, "she's a master at moving stuff an' all."'

'Have her, begod!' exclaimed Father.

'I was too flabbergasted to say much at the time, but I've made up my mind to have a straight talk to George,' said Aunt Aggie.

'Have you, begod!' said Father. 'D'you think that's wise?'

But Aunt Aggie left as abruptly as she'd arrived.

'I've often wished him a pennorth, nuisance as he is, but I'd never have wished her on him,' said Mother.

Several days went by; and almost everybody who came to our house or shop had some comment to make about the strange business of Uncle George and Mrs Aspall.

'I expect they'll want me to play the organ,' said Mrs Peabody, 'but before I do he'll have to take back some of those horrible things he's said about me.'

'Ho! Ho!,' said Micah Elford. 'George have met his master at last, she'll quomp him.'

'He's just like a rabbit waiting for a stoat to pounce on him,' said Reuben Kimmins.

Then Colonel came and told us that he'd seen Aunt Aggie 'marchin' down the strit, 'er face that red you'd think 'er was off to lay an egg.'

'Begod!' exclaimed Father. 'When she looks like that it means she intends to have a barney.'

After we had tea, Father said he thought he'd 'slip down to see Aggie.'

'It's more than I can stand,' complained Mother. 'It's more than flesh and blood can stand, all this George business, this slipping down to Aggie at every whipstitch, all this gossip – it's driving me out of my mind. You'll have two of us out of our minds before you know where you are – that George has already gone.'

'He's not himself, Ethel, old lady.'

'I should be going to W.I. tonight, but how can I? How can I go to the meeting with all this talk? Oh, oh, oh, I wish the great, fat cratur would marry that hussy if he's going to. I wish they'd marry and then go forty thousand miles away.'

'Give me another cup of tea, old lady, before I go.'

*   *   *   *   *

'Go on in and sit down,' said Aunt Aggie, as soon as we arrived. 'I won't be a minute, I'm just getting the old fella some broth. Do you know, when the old fella came home he was bathered right out. I gave him a nice tea, a nice bit of fish – so nourishing, you know, and so good for his poor old brain – and some rice pudding. Then I made him comfy in his chair and he had a little nap. Now he's awake and got a bit peckish – he must keep his strength up – but he's very cheerful now, bless him.'

'Makes you sick, don't it,' muttered Father as Aunt scuttled into the kitchen, leaving us to find our own way into the living room.

'Evening, Sam,' said Father.

'You agen,' said Uncle Sam. 'You be allus here these days.'

'Here you are, old fella,' said Aunt Aggie, coming in with a steaming bowl. 'Have it while it's hot, it'll do you more good while it's hot . . . Sit up a bit, old fella . . . There, that's better, here's a spoon, now put that nice broth in your old tummy.'

'Argh, argh.'

'Chirpy, isn't he,' said Aunt Aggie, turning to us.

'Any news of our George?' asked Father. 'He ain't been near us for days!'

'George, George, George, it's nothing but George, George all the time,' growled Uncle Sam, spluttering broth over his knees.

'I saw him go by in the van yesterday with that Asp, her high and mighty, like Lady Muck. Then Colonel came along and I said "Look at that woman," and he said he'd heard a few things about her. From what he told me – and I'm not a bit surprised – she's not all she should be, she's . . . oh, I can't say, it's not fit . . .'

'Soddem and goodmorrow,' muttered Sam, who now had bits of broth dangling from his moustache.

'Begod!' exclaimed Father.

'Georgie-porgie kissed the girls an' made 'em cry,' cackled Sam, showering broth in all directions.

'It's no laughing matter,' said Father.

'Steady, steady, mind you don't choke, old fella,' said Aunt Aggie, patting the old fella's back.

'Never saw the woman before our George took up with her,' said Father. 'Where does she live?'

'About six miles away, according to Colonel, over at . . .' began Aunt Aggie.

'Soddem and goodmorrow,' said Sam. 'Regular soddem and goodmorrow at her place by all accounts.'

'Begod!' exclaimed Father. 'Our George would never have anything to do with them kinda tricks.'

'Argh, argh,' said Uncle Sam.

'Well, to continue,' said Aunt Aggie. 'I saw George go by again today in the van, but this time he was alone.'

'Thank God for that,' said Father.

'So,' said Aunt Aggie, rather nettled by this interruption, 'I put on my hat and coat . . .'

'Ah!' said Father.

'Argh, argh,' said Uncle Sam.

'So I put on my hat and coat,' repeated Aunt Aggie in firm tones, 'and went straight down to the shop. And there she was, the hussy, behind the counter as bold as brass and as brazen as Jezebel. "Good afternoon, Aggie," she said. The very idea! Aggie indeed, without as much as by your leave. The cheek of it. And me, I've never acknowledged the woman!'

'Did she, begod!'

'Argh, argh, argh.'

'Oh, take the old fella's bowl, his wrists are so weak when he's been bathered. – Well, she looked at me and I looked at her and then she said. "What can I do for you?"' Aunt Aggie paused. 'And I said,' continued Aunt Aggie, "You can stop chasing my brother."'

'Did you begod!'

'"You just stop pestering my brother," I told her. "You get out of this shop, keep out of this village, keep out of the baker's van and my brother's life, or otherwise . . ."' said Aunt Aggie.

'Otherwise?' prompted Father.

'I left then,' said Aunt Aggie.

'Oh,' said Father.

'Soddem,' grunted Sam.

Aunt Aggie's veiled threat may have subdued Mrs Aspall but it did not stop her chasing Uncle George. She was still seen in his shop and garden. Colonel saw her walking round the sheep with Uncle George and reported that she was still busy in Uncle's house.

'A lot of good your Aggie did,' Mother told Father.

'She ain't seen quite so much with our George, and they do say she ain't got so much to say in the shop and she's never on the van now,' reasoned Father.

'Still waters,' replied Mother.

★   ★   ★   ★   ★

A week or ten days went by. I saw Mrs Aspall a few times. Then came a week when Mrs Aspall was not seen in the village. On the following Sunday Uncle George came to lunch; full of the latest murder and all the scandals in *The News of the World*. He discoursed upon doctors, patent medicines, and pigs.

'Our George do seem his old self today,' said Father, following Mother into the kitchen.

Later, when Father and Uncle were drinking tea, Mother asked, 'How's your lady friend, George?'

'Lady friend?' rumbled Uncle George. 'I ain't got no lady friend.'

'Mrs Aspall,' said Mother.

'Oh, her,' replied Uncle in an off-hand manner, 'her's no friend of mine, just someone I gave a lift to when 'twas rainin' cats an' dogs.'

'You appeared to be very friendly,' said Mother.

'An, an' her got too friendly for my likin',' confessed Uncle. 'Well, it got so as I couldn't move without her, her got like a pet lamb, keep follerin' me about. I tried to dodge her times out o' number. I did all manner o' tricks but 'twas no good.

Her told me as her'd lost two husbands an' hadn't a friend in the world an' I felt sorry for her. A few times 'er cried, an' I can't abide women cryin'. Can't stand 'em at any time, funny craturs, women, but they be wuss when they do cry. "I'm all alone, George," 'er'd say. Well, rajah rhubarb, an' damn it all, what was I to do? None of you lot did or said anythin' and I thought to meself, George, me boy, you'm all alone too, damn my rags if I didn't.'

'Begod!' said Father, 'but you was always together.'

'Live and die,' said Mother.

'An' very near the death o' me,' rumbled Uncle George. 'I couldn't seem to move without that 'oman, then 'er got to fussin' an' then 'er got to bossin'. I stood as much as I could, but there comes a time when a man can't allow hisself to be punished unmercifully just on account o' politeness. When 'er started interferin' in the shop I kept quiet. When 'er started muddlin' in me house I said nowt. When 'er chucked dree bottles o' me parsnip wine away, me best parsnip wine an' fully matured too, I was sorely tempted but I held me tongue.'

'Did you, begod!'

'Ah, I did.'

'I don't know how you did it, George,' said Mother, 'I've never known you to hold your tongue.'

'You know me, Ethel.'

'I do, and that's why I'm surprised.'

'But,' continued Uncle George, 'when she told me that pigs was dirty, stinkin' creatures and that I was to get rid o' them, I let rip, damn my rags if I didn't. After that 'er went away an' I'm damn sure her wunt come back.'

That night I heard Father say to Mother, 'Ethel, old lady, for the first time for weeks, I feel meself again.'

Chapter Four
A Dirty Trick

''Pon my soul,' said Uncle George, 'I don't know what to make on't.'

'Don't know what to make of what?' asked Father.

'The whole baggerin' business,' replied Uncle George. 'It's a complete mystery.'

'It certainly is,' agreed Mother.

Uncle George sucked at his pipe, nodded his head, shook his head, wrinkled his brow and rubbed his nose, muttered 'Rajah, rhubarb,' and then put a charcoal tablet in his mouth.

'What's a mystery?' asked Father.

'He's a mystery,' said Mother. 'It's a mystery to me why he's here at this time of night, making faces and swallowing chemicals, it's a mystery he doesn't explode. And now he's making a mystery out of some cock and bull story. It's a mystery . . .'

'It's no cock and bull story, it's a true bill,' said Uncle George, ignoring Mother's other remarks. 'I do a man a kindness an' how he do treat me? – summat shameful. The other day, Blunt, the policeman, he said to me, "George," he said, "you got that little motor, what about taking me out for a day." "Right-ho," I said, "where shall we go?" "Over to the Green Man," he says, "there's a drop of good beer there. It's off my patch, I don't like goin' in the local pubs on account of my job and the landlord over there's a friend of mine. We'll start early an' make a day on't." Well, yesterday – I got young Ron to look after the shop – and off we went, Bob Blunt an' me. We stopped at the Green Man all day – the beer was A1, absolutely fust class. Merry as crickets we were; "Good job there ain't a bobby about," says Landlord laughing. "Ah, tis an' all," said P.C. Blunt, "we're a nice little company, you an' me an' George an' Bert an' Fred there. A man likes to feel settled when he's havin' a drink, he don't like hurryin'

himself." Now that were a bit of sensible talking, we all agreed
about that.

'"Ah," said Blunt, "you're all men after my own heart,
but," – an' here he wagged a finger at us – "they say you can't
trust a policeman." Fred looked a bit startled at this, but
Blunt said, "Don't none of you fear none, we'm all friends
here, just havin' a harmless little drink, doin' no damage to
anything or anybody except that cask o' beer, an' what's more
I be off duty, I be just like the rest of you, a man as likes a
drink."'

Uncle stopped talking, blew out his cheeks and looked hard
at the fire – it was a cold night in November. Father stared at
the fire. Mother went outside and returned with a bucket of
slack coal which she tipped on the fire, effectively smothering
its flames and warmth.

Uncle George continued his story. 'Well, we stopped there
drinkin' an' talkin' until Arthur Gage said it would soon be
time for him to open up. We all laughed at that. "Very good,
very good," said Bob Blunt, putting his hand in a waistcoat
pocket an' bringin' out a watch – why the silly bagger couldn't
have looked at the clock on the wall was a mystery to me – and
said it was time for us to be goin' as he'd have to be on duty
soon.'

'Drink!' snorted Mother. 'Drink, that's all you think about.
Drink and food and murder and illness and gossip.'

'Pigs,' said Father, 'George do think a lot about pigs, don't
you, George?'

'Ah,' replied Uncle George, 'I'd aim as I be the most
thinkin' man about pigs anywhere in these parts or most
nearly anywhere else.'

'The most stinking man of pigs,' said Mother.

'The smell of pigs is like perfoom to me, Ethel. Thur's
nothin' I like better'n to be with pigs.'

'George do love pigs, Ethel, he loves to be with 'em,'
explained Father.

'Birds of a feather,' said Mother. 'Like him and that Blunt.'

'Birds of a very different feather as I be tellin' you, if only
you'd let me. Why people keep int'ruptin' is beyond me, I'm a
man as likes to stick to the point an' get on wi' it. Now, there's
Theo Biddle, he's a master at goin' all the way round – stick to
the point, Theo, I do say to'n.'

'I can't see the point of all this,' said Mother.

'Well, we left the Green Man, Bob Blunt an' me and home we comes, talkin' an' jokin' an laughin', the best of friends, never a cross word. Fact, I was thinkin' to meself what a fust class chap ol' Bob Blunt were tho' he's a bobby. Well, when we comes to the road where you gotta go up around, Blunt says to me, "Pull up, George, it would never do for us to be sin together, not in the state we be in, me bein' a policeman an' all. I'll get out here an' cut up the field, 'tis only a coupla minutes walk, I daresay I'll be in the village sooner'n you, most likely we'll meet each other in the street."

'Well, soak me bob if he weren't right, when I drove into the village, there he were comin' towards me, a bit staggery y'know, but he were a comin'. Well, it were my intention just to wave to him as we passed an' drive on by. But no, as I got closer to him, he stepped out into the road and held his hand up. What do he want, I thought to myself, what 'ave 'e gotta say what he ain't had the chance of all day?

'"George," he says, all solemn like, "where've you been?" I just laughed, but he didn't, he just asked me again where'd I been, an' so I asked him where'd he been. "Oh," he says, "t'ain't no odds where I been, I'm a policeman an' I'm askin' where've you bin." I told him he knew where I'd been and he said that it was no business of mine what he knew, 'twas my business to answer his question.

'Just to humour him, I told him where I'd been, an' he said, "You've bin drinkin' an' atter hours by the seems on't. Now I don't want to be hard on you, so I'll say no more about drinkin' after hours. But . . ." – he was swaying when he said this an' pointed his finger at me – "You're drunk, George." "And so be you," I said and let in the clutch ready to go on – a joke's a joke but thur's no need to make a meal on't.

'"Here, hold hard, George," he says. "You be drunk and in charge of a motor vehicle, I shall have to make a case of this."

'"This is very different talk to that in the Green Man a while back," I said. "Ah," he says, "but I was off duty then," and then puffs out his chest, "but I be on duty now and I shall have to make a case of this." "Case, be damned," I said, "Drunk be damned," I said. "Of course I be drunk, Bob, and so be you, drunk as a wheel you be or you wouldn't be talkin' in this manner o' fashion." But all as he said was, "I'm sorry,

George, but you be drunk in charge of a motor vehicle and I'm a police officer an' duty's duty." I drove off then, there wasn't no use argyfying with the drunken muntle.'

'I expect he was only joking, George,' said Father.

'Jokin' be damned,' replied Uncle, 'that's what I thought until tonight. When I came out of the Lion, I met him coming up the street in his uniform. "How be, Bob," I says to him. "Evenin', George," he says, solemn and official like. "About yesterday," I says, "you almost had me worried, talkin' 'bout makin' a case on't." "'Tis summat to worry about, George," he says, "I don't blame you for bein' worried, 'tis a serious offence bein' drunk in charge of a motor vehicle." "Good job 'twas you what caught me," I says, "or it would be summat to worry about." "It is an' all," he says, "I be worried about it, I don't like to see local people in trouble, 'specially when they be friends of mine. If I was you, I'd see a solicitor." "Solicitor, be dammed," I said, "what do I want with a solicitor." "To defend you in court," he says. "But I bain't goin' to court," I tells'n. "Ho yus, you are," he says. "I've sent in a report."'

'Never,' said Father.

'I'm beginnin' to think he have. He seems set on the idea, I can't understand what have come over him. As I said, it's a complete mystery.'

* * * * *

A few weeks later, Uncle George received a summons to appear in court on a charge of being drunk while driving a motor vehicle.

'The muntle,' said Uncle George, 'he'll be in trouble over this job. Wait 'til I get up in court an' tell 'em that he were as tight as a tick an' produce witnesses to prove it; Arthur Gage an' that Bert an' Fred. That'll make P.C. Blunt smile on t'other side of his face, damn my rags if it wun't.'

'You got him there, George,' said Father. 'He was a silly fellow to make a case of it. It might even get him dismissed from the Force.'

'Serve'n right, too. I tried to reason with'n, I did all I could for his own good but he wouldn't harken.'

'You've got witnesses, George, an' he haven't. It looks pretty black for him.'

'Black as thunder,' agreed Uncle. 'And I'm off to the Green Man straight away to see Arthur Gage. Like to come for the ride, boy?'

'Ah, go with your Uncle,' said Father. 'He needs a bit of company on a job like that.'

'I'd rather he didn't go,' said Mother. 'I don't want him mixed up in anything like this. It'll be bad enough as it is – such a disgrace to the family, it'll be in the paper, everybody will see it, there'll be talk . . . as if we haven't had disgrace and talk enough. If it isn't one thing it's another, I don't think I can stand much more. If my poor father was alive he'd turn in his grave. Well, there's one thing for certain, I shan't be sending my sister, Dorothea, the paper that week. Oh, now look what you've done – my saucepan's boiling over . . .'

This diversion allowed me to escape and accompany Uncle George to the Green Man.

'Back again, George,' said Arthur Gage, all smiles. 'I'm not surprised, it's a drop of good beer I keep here.'

'I'll have a drop while I'm here, it suits me summat wonderful, but that ain't the main reason I'm here,' said Uncle George. Then dropping his voice, 'I've come about summat most pertickler.'

'Most particular. Have you indeed. Now I wonder what that could be?'

'I'm a goin' to tell ye directly. It's most pertickler an' highly confident. I wants to see that Bert an' Fred as well.'

'Most particular an' confident indeed. I'm most interested and I'm sure Bert and Fred will be interested too, both of them are the sort of chaps what like to take an interest in things, particularly confidential business – you see, they likes to have something to talk about, it can get very dull around here, 'specially at this time of year when it gets dark early and light late and in between whiles often damp and foggy. But the trouble is they ain't here, they'll be most upset. But never mind, I'll tell 'em all about it, you may depend.'

Uncle George gave Mr Gage a full, but very rambling account of what had happened – Mr Gage nodded his head and occasionally said 'hum' or 'dear me, dear me.'

'And so,' concluded Uncle George, 'I've come to see you.'

'Very civil of you, very civil indeed. Bert and Fred will be most interested, and they'll talk about it, you may depend.'

'I don't want 'em chopsing all over the place.'

'No, no, of course not and no more do I, it could get me in a bother if it got about that you and the bobby got drunk here, and after hours too. No, no, you can depend upon me, and Bert and Fred, we'll just keep it to ourselves,' said Mr Gage, smiling in a knowing kind of manner.

'You don't quite get my meanin',' said Uncle George, 'I ain't just come all the way over here just to tell you so as you an' that Bert an' Fred can have summat to talk about in the fog. I've come to ask you an' t'other two to come an' be witnesses, to stand up in court, four square an' fearless, an' to testify. To say in no uncertain manner that P.C. Blunt was as tight as a tick, as drunk as a wheel, a greedy, drunken, varmint as have got no business being an officer of the law and persecutin' the likes o' me.'

Mr Gage had stopped smiling and started to frown.

'What's the matter with you?' demanded Uncle. 'Be you in pain, suddenly stricken with summat, neuralgia, belly ache, or what? Tell me what your trouble is an' I may be able to help you, I've got some wonderful remedies back home. Is it wind? Wind can be a bagger. The screws maybe, or is it the gripes? If 'tis the gripes, you be on a winner, I've got some master stuff for that. It's only just come on the market, the papers speak very highly on it. Oh, 'pon my soul, you be lucky if 'tis the gripes. I got some o' that master stuff in me pocket right here. I never go far without takin' some with me, you never know when the gripes might come to you.'

'I ain't got the gripes,' said Mr Gage.

'That's a pity, that is. I could have done you a good turn, and one good turn deserves another . . .'

'Nor yet the screws, belly ache, wind or neuralgia.'

'Well, what have you got or don't you know? If I were you I'd see a specialist, these local doctors ain't much bottle – not when you don't know what 'tis. You go to see 'em to find out what you got an' the fust thing they say is what's the matter with you. See a specialist . . .'

'There ain't nothing the matter with me,' said Mr Gage. 'Now, if you'll excuse me I've got jobs to do, customers to attend to . . .'

'Hold hard a minute,' said Uncle. 'Thur's that business of coming to court.'

'It's difficult . . .'

'No, I'll pick you up, you an' Bert an' Fred. No need to

worry about that. I'll be here about nine o'clock, next Tuesday.'

'I'd like to do it, George, and I'm sure Bert and Fred would like to oblige, but I can't. And as for Bert and Fred, keep 'em right out of it. In fact, I shan't tell 'em nothin' about it at all – to tell you the truth they're too chopsy by half, let 'em hear half a word and 'tis a dozen and all over the place in no time at all.'

'You'll do on your own, Arthur. Better on your own, I shouldn't want t'others anyway, not after what you've told me about 'em. Mind you, I did have me doubts about 'em all along, couple of low bred uns I shouldn't wonder.'

'I'd come, George. I'd come like a shot. Nobody can't say you can't depend on Arthur Gage.'

'Good, I allus knowed you was a fust class chap.'

'But I cannot. I'd lose my licence, sure as eggs got meat. I'm sorry, but there 'tis, a man have got to think of his livelihood,' explained Mr Gage.

Uncle took this set-back very well, his only comment on the way home was; 'It's a blasted baggeroo an' no mistake.'

★   ★   ★   ★   ★

The night before the day that Uncle George was to appear in court, Father said, 'Slip down and see if your Uncle's all right.'

Uncle George was in his kitchen, just putting a cork in a cider jar.

'Hullo, boy, if you'd come five minutes later I'd ha' bin gone, but as you've come afore I've gone, you can come with me.'

'Where are you going, Uncle?'

'Just down to the police station to take P.C. Blunt a little present.'

'Taking him a present?'

'An, why not? You know me, let bygones be bygones, I allus say. Bury the hatchet, no point in harbourin' ill feelings, a man have got his duty to do, and if 'tis dirty duty, that ain't his fault.'

A cold wind blew down the street, Uncle turned up his coat collar and began to whistle.

'Cheerful, ain't you George?' said Alfred Tucker the butcher, coming round the corner. 'Your job's coming off tomorrow isn't it? Got a good solicitor, I hope?'

'Ain't got no solicitor, Alfred. The job's bad enough without bringing solicitors into't,' replied Uncle.

'Proper parky tonight. Too cold to stop talking. Goodnight, George, and good luck tomorrow.'

We arrived at the police station. 'Wait 'til you see Blunt's face when he sees I've brought him a present, boy,' chuckled Uncle.

'Why, hullo, George, didn't think I'd see you tonight,' said a puzzled P.C. Blunt.

'I've just brought you a little present, Bob,' explained Uncle George.

'I hope it isn't a bribe, George, 'cos if it is, it's a serious offence and you're in trouble enough as it is.'

'No, no, no,' rumbled Uncle George, 'just a little present to show there's no hard feelings. Let bygones be bygones, I allus say. I cussed you a bit, I don't mind admitting, but afterwards I thought if a man's got a duty to do he must do it. I respect you, Bob, for doin' yer duty like a man, without fear or favour. I said to meself, Bob Blunt's a credit to the Force, without men like him, where would us law abiding citizens be?'

'It's uncommon generous of you of course, George. Under those conditions I'll be glad to accept, indeed, it would be churlish if I didn't.'

'A drop o' me special, Bob.'

'I'll enjoy a drop tonight, on a night like this a man who has to be out and about needs a drop of something. But I must say it's a surprise, not many would take your attitude. But there, as I've said before, you're one of the best, George.'

'Ah, bury the hatchet I allus say. Mind, I gave it a lot of thought, I said to meself, shall I take Bob a drop o' me special —just to show I bear him no ill will or shan't I. Fust I thought, no, I'm damned if I will an' then I thought 'tis almost Christmas, the season of good will, damned if I don't go and take him a drop o' me special. So, here I be, an' here 'tis, an' the compliments of the season to you, Bob, old chap.'

'I just don't know what to say, George, you've taken me by surprise, 'tis uncommon good of you to have taken it like you have. But as I've allus said, you're one of the best.'

★　★　★　★　★

We wondered next morning how Uncle George was faring at court. Father wished he had gone to give him support. Mother said Uncle George had brought it on his own head and must put up with the consequences. Father kept glancing at his watch and wondering when Uncle would be back. Mother wondered if he would come back or if he would be locked up. Father said Uncle would only get fined, they'd never put him in prison for a little job like that. Not, said Mother if he'd got the sense to keep his mouth shut, but as he'd never had any sense he'd be more likely to abuse the magistrates and land himself in even more trouble. This suggestion was scorned by Father at ten o'clock, at eleven o'clock; at noon he still maintained that Uncle would only be fined lightly. At one o'clock and no sign of Uncle, he began to have a worried appearance. By two o'clock, he was muttering to himself, 'Prison, prison.'

At three o'clock Uncle George's voice could be heard in the street. He was singing 'Good Christian Men Rejoice.'

Mother was in the shop, she'd just brought Father a cup of tea and an aspirin.

'Begod!' exclaimed Father. 'That's our George and he's singing.'

'Catterwauling,' said Mother. 'That means he must be drunk. Will he never learn? Oh, why does he do it?'

Uncle George burst into the shop beaming with pleasure.

'How did you get on, George?' asked Father.

'Case dismissed with a caution,' answered Uncle George.

'Never!' exclaimed Father.

'Luck of the devil,' murmured Mother.

'Oh, it looked black, black as thunder,' rumbled Uncle. 'I admit I was worried. Serious offence they said. Blunt stood up and gave evidence. "As I was proceeding in the late afternoon . . ." Proceeding, be damned, he was wobbling and I was goin' to tell 'em so. But it looked bad, Blunt were layin' it on a thick un, the varmint. And then he went over all peculiar, his face went white and he paused. "Pray, continue," said the chairman, but old Blunt, whiter than ever, just went "oooh, oooh, oooh." And then it happened. Rajah rhubarb, didn't he stink, didn't it make a mess. And Blunt just stood there, white as a sheet and trembling like a leaf. Them as could, left as fast as they could, the magistrates was like a bunch of hens what the fox was at. "What shall we do?" they was asking the clerk.

'Blunt was told to step down and off he waddled lookin' pretty shitten. "Case dismissed," cried the chairman – they'd have dismissed anything and you couldn't blame 'em, it stunk fair roarin' I can tell you. "With a caution," cried the chairman, gettin' to his feet and scurryin' off. "Clear the court," cried the clerk – and it'll take some clearin' I'll warrant.'

'Begod,' said Father, 'I've never heard the like on't.'

'He should 'ave kept me drop o' special 'til Christmas Day,' said Uncle George, 'It was new perry, made outa Blakeneys an' they bain't called shit-britch fer nothing. But Blunt's a gutsy chap, an' that perry's very morish. I suppose I ought've knowed summat like that would happen.'

'Was it wise?' asked Father. 'He'll be after you now.'

'Well, they say one good turn deserves another and I 'spect it's the same with dirty tricks. But as it turned out, Blunt did two dirty tricks. And I reckon it wunt be long afore he's moved from here. He've fouled his nest you could say.'

Chapter Five

Uncle George's Christmas

The week before Christmas was a busy time for Uncle George. Colonel Biggs was killing and plucking geese and cockerels; and Mrs Biggs was dressing them for him. Ron, in the shop, complained that he was run off his feet. When I wasn't helping in the shop or with the bread round, I seemed to be running errands for Uncle George. As for Uncle George himself, he too was fully engaged in his own fashion; in and out of the shop, round and about in the van, up and down to his holding to see how Colonel and Mrs Biggs were getting on, having hushed conversations with Reuben Kimmins, telling Ron 'to look sharp,' searching for further help, gossiping, arguing and continuously running in and out of the Lion.

'Our George,' Father said, 'is rushed off his feet, he tells me he don't know which way to turn.'

To which Mother replied, 'Into the Lion at every whip-stitch.'

There were other complications and hindrances. Micah Elford complained that a baker had no business selling poultry, it was taking the bread out of other people's mouths; to wit Micah Elford's mouth. He even came into the shop to complain about it.

'It ain't good enough, you takin' the bread out of the mouths of them as need it and got a right to it,' he told Uncle George.

'What's talkin' about, Micah? I'm the chap what puts it in thur mouths. There ain't a man, 'oman or child what would have as much as a crust o' bread if it weren't for me. Here I be, workin' meself to a standstill, on all hours of the day an' night – what with one thing an' another – an' bakin', bakin', bakin' – an' when I got plenty more to do besides. I do put meself out, I can tell you – an' out in all winds and weathers deliverin' bread. And why do I do't? Ask yourself a question – it's to see as people have got bread to put in their mouths.'

'That's not what I mean an' you know it,' replied Micah Elford angrily. 'Bread's your business; fish is my business and with fish business goes poultry business, 'specially at Christmas.'

'It don't go very well with stinkin' ole fish . . .'

'Enough of that. I ain't stoppin here . . .'

'I'm glad of that, you're makin' me shop reek of stinkin' . . .'

'I'll have the law on you for defamation . . .'

'I should think twice about that, the law itself tried to have the law on me and see what happened.'

'Very well,' said Micah, 'but I've warned you. And I dare say Alfred Tucker feels the same, it's butcher's business as well as fishmonger's . . .'

'Alfred Tucker ain't complaining – and I'll tell ye for why. If you go and have a look at his shop you'll see some beautiful plump birds in there, and do you know why they be such beautiful birds? They was bred an' reared an' fed by these yur hands.' Uncle George displayed his large hands, fingers and thumbs fully extended, right under Micah's nose.

Micah was momentarily speechless, and Uncle continued, 'Alfred is the sorta chap who only buys an' sells the best, he've told me so himself, many times, only the very best. So, naturally he comes to me for poultry at Christmas. Folk do want a good bird at Christmas, summat what 'ave got some meat on't, summat tender an' juicy, not skin an' bone. So Alfred ain't complainin', he's happy, his customers are happy. And I'll tell ye for why, they get some beautiful birds, not like they scrawny ole things . . . Eh, eh, Micah, you ain't going', I ain't finished yet.'

But Micah Elford left in a hurry, slamming the door behind him. 'I wonder what have upset him,' said Uncle George.

Micah Elford hadn't long been gone when Reuben Kimmins came in. He waited until there were no customers in the shop and then said, 'I've come for the raisins, George.'

'I'll just pop out the back an' get 'em,' said Uncle.

'And a few paper bags,' said Reuben.

'I've got 'em put by, you'll find some honey down at my place – Colonel's down there, he knows where 'tis – now wait a minute – no, come with me an' then you can slip out the back way – at peep o' day, remember, an' mum's the word,' said Uncle George.

When Uncle returned he announced that he had to pop out for a few minutes. Ron was in the bakehouse, so I was left in charge of the shop. Between serving customers I looked around the shelves, under the counter, in the cupboards and drawers – one never knew what Uncle George might have tucked away. On the shelves there were bread, buns, bags of flour, glass-topped tins of biscuits tipped on their sides, and jars of Uncle George's honey, thick chrystalised honey. Why, I wondered, did Reuben have to go down to Uncle's house to fetch honey when there were jars of it in the shop. And paper bags, there were paper bags of several sizes in the shop, but Reuben had to have paper bags which had been put aside. Under the counter was a muddle; empty tins and jars, string, bottles of home-made wine, old invoice books and papers. In the cupboards I found packets of tea, tins of fruit, sardines and mustard, white paper bags, brown paper bags, blue paper bags, orange paper bags, balls of string. There were more bottles of home-made wine, bottles of patent medicines, packets of patent medicines, newspaper cuttings, pig rings, pig powders, an old hat, a cardigan, a couple of Sexton Blake magazines, an air gun and a pair of binoculars. In the drawers there was a jumble of papers, broken bootlaces, money, broken pipes, tins of charcoal tablets, whistles, knives, nails, screws, string, and – as Uncle would say, all manner o' things.

Searching through this treasure trove and attending to customers kept me pleasantly occupied during Uncle's absence which extended to far longer than the promised few minutes.

Ron came in from the bakehouse, covered in flour. 'Isn't he here?' he asked.

'No, he said he had to pop out for a few minutes.'

'That were more than an hour ago. He's always popping out for a few minutes and leaving me to do everything. I say – you goin' carol singing? Do you know – my dad's gettin' a wireless for Christmas. I shan't stop here much longer.'

Ron's ambition was to be a railway porter and he was always saying that as soon as there was a vacancy he'd be off.

Uncle George, red-faced, out of breath and accompanied by an aroma of beer, returned. 'Come on now, lads, don't stand about chatterin', there's plenty to do an' not much time to do't. This is a busy time of the year, we must all put our backs into it. Got the van loaded, Ron?'

'How could I load the van, when I've had everything to do in the bakehouse?' complained Ron.

'Never mind, finish your work in there, I'll see to the van,' said Uncle George. And when Ron had gone, he said, 'I seem to have to do everything, or nothing would get done, but there 'tis, I'm used to it, on the go all the time. Good job I popped out just now, there was old Colonel and Reuben, just sitting down drinking my cider. "Come on, Colonel," I said, "you should be pluckin' them cockerels, and as for you Reuben, you got plenty to do, and if you ain't you can kill them cockerels over there –" he's a master at killin' birds, kills 'em right dead you know, no messin' about. What a good job I popped down, that Colonel, he'd been tearin' some of my lovely cockerels – I spoke sharply to him, he'll be more careful now. And on me way back I saw a chap I wanted to see most pertickler, just goin' into the Lion, so I went in atter him. What a good job I did, I saw several in there I wanted to see most pertickler, saved me no end o' runnin' about, catchin' em all in there together. Now, come on, we can't stand about, there's the van to be loaded, the hoss to harness. We'll have to have a bite of bread an' cheese as we do go along.'

Next morning when I went into the shop, Uncle George wasn't there. Ron told me he hadn't seen Uncle all morning, explaining that the night before he'd been given the shop keys with instructions to arrive early. Again I took charge of the shop while Ron busied himself elsewhere. About ten o'clock Uncle arrived. 'Not long to Christmas now. We've a busy day ahead of us, 'pon my soul, I've already had a busy day.'

We had a busy day, Ron and I, and even Uncle George when he was there, but he did have to keep 'popping out.' And if he wasn't popping out, Alfred Tucker was popping in and having whispered conversations with Uncle George. Reuben came for more raisins. Colonel came and complained that his fingers were raw, but he cheered up when Uncle suggested a visit to the Lion. Aunt Aggie came for some lardy cakes, and told me that Uncle Sam was being rushed off his feet and that Mrs Peabody had been quite abusive to the poor old fella because he had not finished decorating her kitchen, but what could she expect, Sam had only started on it three weeks ago. Cheerful customers came, doleful and complaining customers came, Uncle George came and went and eventually returned.

It was, as I said, a busy time, especially with all the coming and going. Ron made veiled remarks about going too, and noises which I supposed were meant to resemble the noise of trains coming and going. Eventually the daylight went and darkness came; Uncle shut up the shop and Uncle, Ron and I went our separate ways.

The next day, I almost didn't go to the bakery. Mother said there was plenty for me to do at home; there were sticks to chop, coal to be carried and a dozen other things to be done, she was working her fingers to the bone, and say what we would, she couldn't be expected to do everything. Furthermore, my Father could do with my help in the shop. So I chopped sticks, carried coal and then Mother complained that I was under her feet and Father said I'd better go and give Uncle George a hand as Uncle had said he could hardly cope with all he had to do, he was that busy he didn't know which job to do first.

Two days before Christmas, when I went to fetch the horse, Colonel and Mrs Biggs were busy plucking pheasants over bowls of water. While we were hitching the horse to the baker's cart I remarked upon it to Uncle.

'Mum's the word, boy,' he said, putting a finger to his nose.

'But why the bowls of water?' I asked.

'To stop the feathers blowin' everywhere an' makin' a mess.'

'But there's goose feathers and cockerel feathers blowing everywhere.'

'Pheasant feathers be different and mum's the word. You mustn't mention pheasants to anyone, not even to me. You see, pheasants be game, an' it would be a game if people got to hear. Coveteous people like ole Micah 'specially. He ain't got game to sell and he'd like to have an' if he knew I had he'd get me into a bother. You see, I ain't got a licence to sell game – it ain't worth me gettin' one, not just to sell a few little pheasants, just at Christmas. I don't really know why I bother with it, but you know me, I'll tell ye for why, some folk do like a little pheasant at Christmas and so I put meself out just to oblige 'em. Only certain people mind, them what be pertickler and don't like pheasants all full of shot. And you can depend upon it, they wun't find no shot in my pheasants, I'm very pertickler about that. But as I said, mum's the word, it don't do to let people know everything. It ain't wise to let some on 'em know anything, P.C. Blunt f'rinstance. Never let him know anything, 'cos when he do he only makes a mess on't, the dirty varmint. But us wun't have much more bother from him, he'll be going soon after Christmas.'

'I see, Uncle George.'

'You mean you ain't seen anything like?'

'Mum's the word, Uncle.'

'You're a sharp boy. I can see you see what I mean.'

Nearly everything was sharp on the morning of Christmas Eve. There was a sharp frost, and a sharp wind blowing down the street. Uncle said he'd been up and about bright and early and had made a sharp start to the day. He told Ron and me to 'look sharp,' and announced that he felt 'as sharp as a razor.'

'We must,' he declared, as he bustled about the shop, 'make a sharpish start on the round, there's a lot to do, no time for dallying about, sharp's the word this morning.'

Ron said he wanted to finish sharp because he was going carol singing and Uncle said that would be all right, he'd a mind to go carol singing too.

'Sharp un this morning,' said Reuben as he came into the shop. Reuben was coming on the round today as there was also the poultry to be delivered. 'I've put the hoss in the van,' he said.

'The bread's in there ready, so we'll get off,' announced Uncle George. 'Shut the shop sharp at five, Ron, if we ain't back, but we'll be back afore then, I'll warrant.'

We drove down to Uncle George's house to get the poultry. Mrs Biggs helped us to load it in the van; geese, cockerels, and pheasants – the pheasants received special attention, they were carefully wrapped and placed well out of sight. 'Well done, Mrs Biggs,' said Uncle, 'you've made a capital job. Now for the bottles, steady with 'em.'

Colonel, I learnt, was delivering a few beautiful birds in the village and would attend to Uncle's livestock that afternoon.

'Colonel's a fust class chap, a dependable chap, most reliable,' said Uncle George, when all the bottles were stowed carefully in the van. 'And Mrs Biggs is a good 'oman. And you're a fust class chap, Reuben. And me nephew's got all the makings of one, and I'm a fust class chap, damn my rags if I b'aint. We're all a good happy little band, and there ain't a man jack among us as don't know how to keep things to hisself. And I tell ye for why, we ain't coveteous like some, that's why. Go and have a glass or two of port in the Lion on me, Mrs Biggs, and a happy Christmas to you. Hold on a minute, while I slip into the house . . .'

Uncle returned wearing a bowler hat and a frock coat. 'Now we're ready,' he announced. And off we went at a spanking pace. 'The old horse is right sharp this morning,' said Uncle George.

'Sharp's the word this morning,' said Reuben.

Down the street we went, along the lanes . . .

'The old horse do go, don't he,' said Reuben.

'Christmas comes but once a year,' said Uncle.

'There's something I'd like to know,' I said.

'Well, ask away,' said Uncle.

'Why did Mr Kimmins have to go down to your house to get honey and why did you have to get paper bags for him when there was plenty of honey and paper bags in the shop?'

''Twas runny honey at the house and you need sweet bags, pointed 'uns,' replied Uncle.

'Them's trade secrets, mind,' said Reuben.

'Ah, mum's the word,' said Uncle George.

A clear stretch of the road lay ahead of us, its verges crisp and white and sparking in the sunlight. The horse shook its head as if for very joy; the harness rattled, chains jingled, the wheels of the van seemed to skim over the surface of the road. The keen, cold air bit at our faces, giving them a glow and a colour.

'He do fair goo this morning,' said Reuben.

'Like one o'clock,' said Uncle George.

After a while, Reuben said, 'Bit nippy, ain't it.'

'There's a bottle of sloe gin right by your elbow, Reuben. We'll have a drop. I put it in special for us, seeing as it were a sharp morning.'

We each had a swig from the bottle and I think my two companions would have had more swigs, but we'd already arrived at a group of houses.

'No hanging about, mind. Just give 'em their stuff an' on to go,' instructed Uncle. 'A bottle o' plum an' a goose at one, just bread at another, cockerel and parsnip wine – it's cheap at the price I'm askin' . . .'

*   *   *   *   *

At some houses we only took bread, at others we took geese, cockerels or pheasants, at some bottles of home-made wine. Some customers gave us mince pies, some gave us 'a spot of something'. Long before we finished Uncle George and Reuben must have had enough spots I wondered they didn't begin to look like leopards. At every stop we made Uncle George begged Reuben and me 'not to hang about, but to look sharp.' Neither Reuben nor I did hang about which was more than could be said for Uncle George.

At mid-day Uncle George produced thick sandwiches which were filled with fat bacon and a liberal amount of mustard which we ate as we travelled. And after almost every stop Uncle remarked, 'Just behind us are the most beautiful, plump birds anyone ever did see.'

Occasionally he varied his remarks. 'The most magnificent birds human eyes did ever see an' the tastiest birds human teeth will ever champ, I'll warrant. Not as they'll need any champing, they be that tender.' Or, 'It does me heart good to see 'em, 'pon my soul, if it don't. Colonel and his missus have made a pretty good job of 'em too. Colonel's a master plucker, damned if he ain't, and his missus do dress 'em a treat.'

Of the pheasants he said, 'Nice little birds an' not a bit o' lead in 'em. How many did we have, Reuben, an' not a shot fired? – well, 'tis no matter.'

We came to a farm and a couple of cottages. Uncle clambered down and produced a nose-bag filled with chaffed hay for the horse. 'No need to be in too much of a hurry, the horse have got to have his victuals,' he said. Reuben went to one cottage, I to the other, while Uncle made for the farmhouse.

I returned, Reuben returned, we stood and waited and stamped our feet. The horse finished its victuals and still Uncle George did not return.

'This is his trouble,' Reuben said, 'he will stop and talk.'

At last he appeared, his face as red as the beetroot of which he was so fond. 'Be you ready, lads?' he asked, 'Let's get a move on, we've a lot to do and a long way to go yet.'

Cups of tea and mince pies, talk and laughter were enjoyed by Uncle, Reuben and me. Our stock of bread, poultry and bottles went down as the red sun sank in the west.

'Not a shot in 'em,' Uncle George muttered from time to time.

The air became more chilly, we had some more bacon sandwiches and another drop of sloe gin. When dusk came upon us, our customers stopped serving tea and began to offer 'a little spot of something.' The lamps on the van were lighted and after more 'little spots' Uncle George began to sing:

'Christmas comes but once a year
And it's everyone's job to keep it up, keep it up.
Strolling round the town, knocking the people down,
Rare old, fare old, rickety, rackety crew . . .'

More deliveries, more mince pies, more 'little spots,' more gossip and laughter. The moon was now shining and Uncle George and Reuben sang:

'It's my delight on a shiny night . . .'

The air became colder and we all sang:

'Sire, the night is darker now
And the wind grows stronger
Fails my heart I know not how,
I can go no longer.'

With great power Uncle bellowed, 'Bring me flesh and bring me wine.'

After several more stops and a few more 'spots', both Uncle George and Reuben grew less steady on their feet but much merrier. They seemed to find getting in and out of the van more difficult and the further we went the more they laughed. Then we lost Uncle George, one minute he was walking round the van and just about to climb in and the next he was gone.

'George! George!' shouted Reuben, 'where are you?'

No answer came. 'Funny,' said Reuben, 'there he was by my side and now he's gone – vanished.'

'Uncle! Uncle!' I shouted, feeling rather alarmed.

'George! George! Where be you?'

No answer.

'This is a rum un,' said Reuben.

'Help! Help!' we heard, coming from we knew not where.

'Where be you?' shouted Reuben.

'I don't know where the hell I be,' answered Uncle.

Neither did we. Although we searched we could not find him, but again we heard, 'Help, help, you damned nogmen.'

'Where be you, George?' asked Reuben.

'I be here now. I was there until it happened.'

We found him in a hole and helped him out. 'If you was just there, George, you was bound to hear us when we fust shouted,' said Reuben.

'Of course I heard you. I ain't deaf,' retorted Uncle.

'Why didn't you answer then?'

'I couldn't. Fallin' down there knocked all the breath out of me.'

'You all right now?'

'Ah, I'm all right now, but 'twere a terrible sensation, I thought the earth was swallering me up. Many's the time I've wished it would, when I've bin in a bit of a bother like. I shall have to have a drop though, to steady me nerves. I don't mind tellin' you I thought it were the end of me.'

'I'd better have a drop too,' said Reuben. 'That job have upset my nerves. I don't mind tellin' you, I thought we'd sin the last o' you. You never know, you do hear tell of such funny things happening.'

''Twern't funny, Reuben.'

'It is, George, when you come to think on't.'

'I've a good mind to shove you down thur, so's you can have a bit of fun, Reuben.'

'I'm gettin' enough fun without gettin' down holes to get it, George.'

'Ah, you can laugh an' gyule, folk have no business leavin' holes about in the dark. I could have broke me neck fallin' down there.'

''Taint much of a hole, George, 'tis more of a ditch I expect, if we could see it rightly.'

'So it's all right if it's a bit of a ditch like, is it? A man mustn't complain if he falls in an' breaks his neck an' dies a long lingerin' death or even a short horrible un.'

'I didn't say that, George,' reasoned Reuben. 'And you didn't break your neck.'

'No, I didn't break me neck, but I might have. I daresay most nearly anybody else would, 'cos it ain't many as would have the sense to fall as I did. Not if they was called upon to fall sudden and unexpected, you can't expect everyone's wits to work quick in a 'mergency like mine do.'

'If your wits be all that quick, George, 'tis a mystery how you came to fall in the hole in the fust place.'

'How can your wits be quick about nothin'? That were the trouble. I stepped into nothin'. No man, not even me, can cope with nothin', if it's summat that's diff'rent, I can most allus cope with summat, it's nothin' what foxes me.'

'I can't see that, George.'

'No, and I couldn't see that hole, reckon it must 'ave bin six, – no more likely ten foot deep.'

Our arrival at some more houses broke up this discussion on holes. A few more stops, a great deal of gossip and a few more 'spots' and then the last loaf of bread was delivered, the last goose, pheasant and cockerel and the last of the bottles delivered. The last bacon sandwich eaten, the last drop of sloe gin drunk, another song was sung and we were rumbling through our village. 'A merry Christmas,' we called to everyone we saw. Back at Uncle George's the horse was led into the stable and unharnessed. 'Well done, ole fellow,' said Uncle George, patting the horse. 'Well, that's that, the end of a hard day.'

'We've missed the carol singing,' said Reuben.

'So we have,' said Uncle, 'but we've been hard at it all day. It's chaps like us what keep the spirit of Christmas going. Well, boy, you'd better get off home to your mother or she'll be wondering where you are. Me and Reuben are goin' to the Lion for a drink, we've earned it y'know.'

* * * * *

Uncle George came for Christmas dinner as he always did. And as usual he'd been to see Aunt Aggie. 'A merry Christmas, I said to Sam, but what's the good, he don't know the meanin' of the word, Christmas or no Christmas. I wonder how our Aggie do put up with him.'

'By gum,' said Father at dinner, 'this is a good goose of yours, George.'

'Ah, he was the best o' the lot, but they was all good.'

'By gum,' said Father, 'this is a good pudding, Ethel, old lady.'

Uncle George was rather subdued. He said the last week's exertions had tired him no end.

'And the drink,' muttered Mother.

'But,' continued Uncle George, 'Christmas comes but once a year . . .'

'By gum,' said Father, 'you're right, George.'

'And quite often enough,' murmured Mother.

'And,' said George, 'it's up to us to keep it up.'

'And down as much as you can, food and drink,' muttered Mother.

'But it have told on me this year, I shall have to go quietly for a bit,' said Uncle George. 'I've been hard at it, night an' day, in all winds and weathers. Besides, there was that court case as well. I say – I wonder if Blunt saved a drop of me special to have with his Christmas dinner?'

On Boxing Day Uncle George just looked in and told us he was going over to the Green Man. 'I'm takin' Reuben and Colonel with me, they're damn good chaps, I don't know how I'd have managed without 'em. Besides, I'd like to see Arthur Gage an' that Bert an' Fred, they ain't bad chaps. I've got a few things to tell 'em, they like to talk things over afterwards especially if there's any fog about and I daresay they'd like to have summat to talk about if we get some snow.'

'Boxing Day,' said Mother, 'is boozing day for some, but for him every day's a boozing day. I don't know why he makes such a fuss about Christmas.'

A few days later, apropos of nothing, Uncle George said, 'I hear the syndicate didn't have much of a time on Boxing Day, by all accounts they hardly saw a pheasant.'

Chapter Six

Mainly about Pigs

Fortune had smiled on Uncle George recently; as he would have said, 'things had turned up trumps.' He'd rid himself of Mrs Aspall, he turned the tables on P.C. Blunt, he'd managed to annoy Micah Elford over the Christmas poultry business, he'd 'put one over' the hated shooting syndicate, giving them 'one in the eye' and making a 'tidy penny' too. In case anyone is still wondering how he managed to obtain dozens of pheasants 'without a shot in 'em', perhaps I should explain that pheasants love raisins, and if the raisins happen to be in a pointed paper bag, well smeared on the inside with sticky honey – but as Reuben said, 'it's a trade secret,' so mum's the word.

Now with the cold days of January we entered a period of tranquility; 'the dull time of the year' as Uncle George always called the weeks after Christmas. Those beloved pursuits of his, the cider and the wine making were over; even the garden was dull at this time of year. There was the bakery of course, but bread was not and never had been very exciting for him. The delivery round still provided gossip, a few trivial incidents, but in the main, even the round succumbed to this period of dullness. Nobody wanted advice on gardening, no one, not even Uncle, wanted to stand around outside at this cold time, talking at length and staring at gardens or fruit trees, or gaze meditatively for very long over a wall at a pen of pigs, even the pigs didn't come out to be gazed at, no matter how fondly. The pigs preferred to stop huddled in a warm nest of straw in their low sties – and Uncle George was not built for prolonged bending. It was, said Uncle 'a dull time, the time for warm cider with ginger in it.'

On a Sunday morning in January we were sitting in the garden shed; Uncle and I, Colonel and Reuben – Uncle held court some Sunday mornings in the shed. 'It's a quiet time,' said Uncle, tipping a little ginger into the saucepan of cider on top of the stove and then stirring it with his forefinger. 'A quiet time,' Uncle repeated, 'but I'm glad on't after all the hustle and bustle, but before we can look round Easter'll be on us, and before I know where I am I'll be up to me eyes. There'll be all the work in the garden; all manner of advice to give to people round about, they'll be clamourin' for't. It'll be George this an' George that, what shall I do an' when shall I do't. Mind, I don't begrudge 'em, those who got the sense to ask for advice. It's them as wun't ask, or take it when 'tis given what zasperates me, an' they're the ones what takes up the time. An' then thur's all the work with hot cross buns, folk do clamour for my hot cross buns, mind, you con't blame 'em, they'm good buns, the best buns money can buy, but they're work, you con't make buns like mine without a fairish ol' bit o' work. But – to tell you the truth, I'm gettin' fed up with this bakery business.'

'I'm gettin' fed up with business too,' complained Colonel, 'it ain't all profit. Back last autumn I sold a chap one of me ferrets an' I've never had the money. I've axed him time an' agen but him wun't pay.'

'Some on 'em wun't pay, I do know that,' rumbled Uncle.

'No,' said Colonel, 'this chap wun't pay.' Colonel paused and after a few minutes contemplation said, 'If I'd ha' knowed he weren't goin' to pay, I'd ha' charged him twice as much.'

'That wouldn't have bin sufficient,' said Uncle very decisively. 'That wouldn't have bin enough, not to cover your overheads an' all – to say nothing of the debt itself. If you'd ha' known he weren't goin' to pay, never pay, you oughta have asked him more than double what you did.'

'You mean to say I undercharged him more than double what I did?' asked Colonel, looking very worried indeed.

'That's what I'm sayin', more or less,' agreed Uncle. 'What do you say Reuben?'

'I reckon you'm about right, George.'

'It's wuss than I thought,' said Colonel. 'A downright wusser than I thought an' I be a lot wusser off than I thought I was. I'd thought I'd lost five bob at first, by now it seems I've lost a quid. Almost a wik's wages, it's surprisin' how I can manage to live.'

'You got any more young ferrets to sell, Colonel?' asked Uncle.

'No.'

'Thank God fer that, if you'd had any more an' made more deals like that un you've alluded to, it would have bin ruination for you.'

'I've losses enough, I wonder how I stand it, with not much work about an' precious little money comin' in. Thur's the money I'm payin' out reg'lar on me mother-in-law fr'instance.'

'What's up with her, she in debt or summat?' asked Uncle, re-filling the saucepan with cider and adding some ginger.

'No,' replied Colonel, 'but I shall be. A good many years ago I insured her, seemed a good job at the time. Of course, I didn't know she were goin' to live this long, and I bin payin' out reg'lar, reckon I shall lose money on the job.'

'You can never tell with women, they'll most nearly always let you down,' said Uncle George.

'Who's that man what's come to live over in Haycroft Lane?' asked Reuben.

'Dr Fenton,' said Uncle. 'Leastways, he says he's a doctor, but he don't do any doctoring.'

'Perhaps he's retired,' suggested Reuben.

'He ain't that old,' replied Uncle. 'Leastways, he ain't doddery. It's my belief he've bin struck off, reckon he musta done summat pretty terrible. Only a little runt of a chap, bit of a squint, don't reckon he can have bin much bottle as a doctor, good job he bin struck off.'

'Don't Dr Higgins know?' asked Colonel.

'If he do, he wun't say, close as oysters doctors be. But you may depend on't, that little runt have done summat terrible.'

'P.C. Blunt ain't gone yet,' said Reuben.

'No, but he'll be goin' soon, stands to reason,' said Uncle, 'He'll never live down that little job he went and did in court. He'd never be able to take a case there agen, the magistrates 'ouldn't stand for't. No, no, they'd never have him in their court agen for fear he'd let loose agen. Once a fella have had the effrontery to do a nasty trick like that in public, you con't trust him. Besides, even the kids do gyule at him now; he'll be goin' afore many more wiks have passed.'

'There's a chap goin' round buyin' furniture,' said Colonel. 'Mostly ol' stuff, the older the better, they do say he'll give good money for't if 'tis really old. An' if it's got worm holes in it out comes a wad of notes. Seems daft to me, who'd want worm-ridden ol' stuff – but thur, he comes from the town an' there's no accountin' for that sort.'

'I might have some old stuff,' said Uncle George reflectively, 'and if I ain't I reckon I could soon lay me hands on some.'

'I don't like the sound o' that doctor fella,' said Colonel. 'S'pose Higgins was laid up an' he come round an' started killin' us.'

'He con't do that, not if he bin struck off,' said Uncle George.

'But if he ain't bin struck off, we'd be in mortal danger,' said Colonel.

'Of course,' said Uncle, 'I shouldn't just buy worm eaten ol' stuff or people 'ould smell a rat.'

★   ★   ★   ★   ★

Uncle George kept pigs in an old fashioned way; in the summer they ran in the orchard and farrowed in roughly made hovels. In the winter they were housed in snug low roofed sties with open yards. He fed them on chat potatoes bought from a local farmer, on surplus vegetables, barley meal and waste from the bakery. He did not weigh or ration their food in any way, they were fed to appetite, clean troughs and contented pigs were his yardsticks. The potatoes were cooked, the meal was steeped in water with a little fishmeal added. In addition, the pigs were given, as necessary, worm powders, glauber salts and the 'nothing less than magical' pig powders. In summer the pigs grazed the orchards, in season they ate windfall plums, apples and pears; comfrey, the residue from cider making, swedes or mangolds. Their dung was the basis of his success with fruit and vegetable growing.

In summer he spent a long time leaning on the orchard gate looking at his pigs; in winter he leant on the wall of the sties looking at them. Both gate and wall being just the right height to allow a man to lean on them in comfort and gaze with delight. And if he should have a companion to lean with him and gaze and admire, his delight was doubled.

There are all kinds of pigs, as Uncle George never tired of saying, just as there are all kinds of people. There are pigs that grow and fatten quickly and those that don't – good doers and poor doers. If only doctors kept pigs Uncle was wont to say, they would understand there are good doers and poor doers, people whom nature intended to be fat and people whom nature intended to be thin. 'It ain't natural,' he would say, 'it's flying in the face of nature to try and make fat uns thin, it's dangerous, it weakens their constitution and makes 'em the prey to all manner o' illness an' disease. Take me f'rinstance, I be well covered and I d'aim to remain well covered as nature meant me to be. I don't yut to kill meself, I just have me normal amount of vittals 'cos I respect me constitution. Y'see, I'm a good doer. Now old Sam, he's a poor doer, look at him, thin and scrawny, though he do yut an' yut fit to kill hisself. And it ain't as if he's active like me. He's that slow, it's a wonder the paint don't dry on his brush while he's using it. The chap's bone idle, he'll never wear out, he'll rust out. But look at the grub he put's inside him and still he's as thin as a pike handle. But I'm not thin although I'm on the go all the time, all hours of the day an' night, in all winds and weathers.'

There are well behaved pigs and badly behaved pigs, docile pigs and fierce pigs, clean pigs and dirty pigs. Some pigs always kept their beds clean and dunged in a corner of the outside yard. Other bunches of pigs continually fouled their beds – this sort Uncle always referred to as 'sooner pigs.' Mother once asked him what 'sooner pigs' were and he replied, 'Them what 'ould sooner lie an' shit in their beds than take the trouble to go outside.'

At this Mother reddened and said 'That's a filthy word.'

'Ah,' said Uncle George, 'an' it's a filthy job doin' it in their beds an' I've gotta keep takin' the dirty straw out an' puttin' in fresh an' then they goes and does it again. Other pigs keep their beds clean, one lot o' straw'll last 'em for wiks an' they keep warm an' clean.'

Some pigs had good appetites and licked their troughs clean. Others were poor eaters and needed doses of pig powder and the like in order to whet their appetites and to give them a bloom. Some pigs were noisy, some were quiet. Pigs, in a manner of speaking were very much like people, said Uncle George, and if only doctors could be persuaded to keep pigs they would be able to treat and understand their patients better. 'In fact,' he did say, 'doctors oughta have to keep pigs for a year or two before they qualified. There should be pigs at every medical college, in fact, I'd go further and say that every doctor should be made to keep a pen o' pigs when they're in practise on their own account. Higgins oughta have some, an' I've told him so. An' he've got no excuse, 'cos he've got me on hand to advise him.'

'We've got,' replied Mother, 'a baker stinking of pigs and we don't want a doctor stinking of pigs.'

'It mightn't be a bad idea for parsons to kip pigs as well. Bence could keep 'em, he've got plenty o' room at the vicarage. Reuben could soon knock up a little sty an' I'd be there like a shot to give him advice, damn my rags if I 'ouldn't. Good ol' chap, the vicar, 'twould be a pleasure to put him in the way o' pigs.'

'Pigs,' continued Uncle after a pause for contemplation, 'be educational. Policeman oughta keep pigs. Not Blunt, mind you, he ain't a proper person to be in charge o' pigs – or anything else for that matter. Anyway, 'tis no good him havin' pigs, he'll be off it directly. An' another thing, come to think on't he's a sooner-bred hisself.'

Pigs, you will have gathered, were a passion with Uncle George. On that Sunday when things were dull, when Uncle was flush with the profits of poultry and pheasants and home-made wine and with 'hot cider with ginger in it,' what was more natural than his mind turning to the thoughts of pigs. Not so much his mind turning to thoughts of pigs – it never being far from the thoughts of pigs anyway – especially with a sty vacated by pigs sent to market just before Christmas, but to more pigs.

'I've a mind to buy some pigs,' he told Father on that afternoon when the *News of the World* had only provided a meagre crop of scandals and not one advertisement of any remedy which could be called new or hardly short of miraculous.

'Pigs,' said Father in a tone which implied that pigs and the purchase and keeping of pigs was some entirely new venture for Uncle George.

'Pigs,' snorted Mother 'the place would be inundated with pigs if you had your way, what with the doctor, the vicar, and the policeman keeping pigs.'

'You oughta keep a pig, Ethel,' said Uncle George, 'you'd enjoy feeding a pig.'

'I think I already do. He comes here every Sunday, he wanders in here at almost every whipstitch and eats me out of house and home and leaves the place stinking of pigs, but I don't enjoy it.' said Mother.

'Put the kettle on, Ethel, old lady,' said Father, 'we could do with a cup o' tea.'

'What was Ethel alludin' to?' asked Uncle, looking puzzled when Mother had left the room.

'I'm not sure, George, women say a lot what takes some understanding. But never mind that, you were saying something about buying pigs.'

'Oh, ah,' said Uncle George, brightening, 'so I was. Harold Gubbins have got some young Gloucester Spots, some master uns by all accounts, if Colonel's anything to go by. Old Colonel ain't a bad judge of pigs, he've got an eye for a pig, I'll say that for 'im, but he ain't got no idea how to feed 'em, that's his trouble. Just between ourselves – don't let it go any further mind, but I'd like them Spots if I could get 'em at the right price. I don't say I'm desperate for 'em but I'd like 'em if they be as Colonel says they be – and I expect they be if he says so. Master pigs, he said, the whole bunch of 'em. I could fatten the hogs and keep the hilts for breeding. Not a runt among 'em, Colonel said. Now that denotes good breedin' I'll warrant.'

'Fancy that,' said Father.

'Ah, an' I do fancy 'em no end.'

'Not a runt among 'em,' said Father, visibly impressed.

'There's a runt of a fella come to live in Haycroft Lane,' said Uncle George, 'calls hisself a doctor, but he ain't doin' any doctorin' by all accounts. I'd aim he've done summat terrible an' got struck off. I'm not surprised, he've got an evil look about him, but I am surprised we haven't heard about him in the *News of the World*. Still, I expect he've got an assumed name, several names I shouldn't wonder, those sort o' chaps always have a bag o' names, that's how they get away with it for so long. But in the end they catch up with 'em, after they've done a heap o' damage. He've got a shifty look, dare say he's in hiding, livin' in fear an' dread 'til they pounce on him an' take him away an' lock him up.'

'What do you think he's done?' said Father.

'Oh, I don't know, any manner o' things . . .'

'He's a perfectly respectable gentleman,' put in Mother, who had returned. 'Mrs Peabody says he's a very nice respectable gentleman with money.'

'Whatever do Mrs Peabody know about respectable,' said Uncle. 'How can she be a judge on't when her's always runnin' off to the spinney to meet that fancy chap o' hers.'

'I'm not stopping here to hear you say such things about Mrs Peabody,' retorted Mother. 'I'm going to put on my hat and coat . . .'

★　★　★　★　★

When we set off on the bread round on Saturday morning, Uncle George said, 'don't let any of 'em hinder you today, just give 'em the bread an' get from 'em. Some on 'em'll keep you while they talk a donkey's hind leg off if you let 'em. If they ask you to have a cup o' tea or summat, thank 'em politely, but say no. Y'see I've gotta bit of business on today, I want to slip down to Gubbins to buy them Spots. Reuben 'ave seen 'em an' Tucker, the butcher, 'ave seen 'em an' they both said they be master pigs. An' from what Tucker says he don't expect a lot for 'em either, an' I've more or less fixed up with Owen Tishforth to fetch 'em tomorrow mornin'.'

Later, Uncle George told me he had seen the pigs himself, he'd happened to be going by and as the sty was by the road and he wasn't going very fast, he'd happened to glance over the wall, well actually he had happened to stop for a moment and he had just had a quick look at them. Perhaps if Mr Gubbins had been about . . . but being market day when he had, by the merest chance, been going that way, Mr Gubbins was nowhere to be seen. Uncle had not stopped a moment but it had been long enough to see the pigs were indeed 'master Spots'.

Uncle George was less successful than I in preventing the customers from hindering him. 'Try as I would,' he explained repeatedly, 'I couldn't get away. They've got this to say an' that to say and I've more or less got to hear 'em out. It tries me patience, but you've gotta be polite. When they press me to have a drop of summat, it do hurt 'em to say no. Some of 'em do take it as a criticism of their cider if I refuse.'

By mid-afternoon we were driving down the lane to Mr Gubbins' farm. It was not on Uncle's round and was, in fact, rather an out of the way place; not I should have thought the kind of place one would happen to be just passing as Uncle had done earlier in the week.

We drove into the farm yard, scattering a score of ducks and a flock of hens, disturbing a trio of geese. We dismounted; ducks quacked, hens squawked, geese hissed and a sheep dog barked.

'No need to ring a bell here,' observed Uncle George. Mrs Gubbins appeared at the farmhouse door, wiping her floury hands on her apron. Seven cats came and looked at us, two puppies came and growled at our heels, the barking dog strained at its chain. Five children of varying sizes came scampering round the corner of a shed, they stopped when they saw us and stood in a tight group to stare at us. Two farmworkers paused in their work to lean on their forks to regard us with baleful unblinking eyes. A horse in the stable put its head over the door and whinnied, an unseen bull bellowed; several cows and calves did their best to welcome us.

'Don't expect they see many down here,' said Uncle George. 'I expect our visit's a bit of excitement for 'em all.'

Finally, Mr Gubbins, clad in tweed hat, brown smock, breeches, leggings and boots, came ambling towards us.

'Afternoon, George,' he said.

'Afternoon, Harold,' said George.

'Like a drop of cider?' asked Mr Gubbins.

We were taken into a dark shed which contained several cider barrels, up-turned fruit boxes, old coats, cider mats, buckets, fruit baskets, empty sacks, a pile of firewood, a sawing horse, two or three saws and an axe. We sat upon the boxes while Mr Gubbins bent low over a barrel and filled a large, grimy mug with cider.

'Try that,' ordered Mr Gubbins, handing the filled mug to Uncle. Uncle George drank, smacked his lips and pronounced the cider absolutely Al.

'Thought you'd say that,' said Mr Gubbins, looking pleased.

'I'm a master judge of cider,' said Uncle, 'I know a drop of good when I taste it, an' mark my words that is a drop of good, damn my rags if it ain't.'

The mug was passed to Mr Gubbins, then back to Uncle, occasionally to me with the warning 'only a drop mind, its proper powerful stuff.' In this fashion the mug was emptied and refilled several times. Uncle and Mr Gubbins talked about the weather, of acquaintances, the iniquities of the government, of crops and stock, mud and muck, of days they had seen, how times had altered. At last Mr Gubbins asked

Uncle what had brought him that way, on this day of all days.

'I were passing close by and what with almost finishing deliveries an' having half an hour to spare, I thought to meself, I haven't seen Harold for quite a time, I'll pop down an' see how he's farin'.'

'Very civil on you, George, and I do appreciate it. We don't see many down here, not at this time o' year. A few drops in from time to time for a chat an' a tot, but that's all.'

Then to my amazement, Uncle George said, 'I also wondered if you was lookin' for a bunch o' pigs.'

'Pigs, George, pigs?' said Mr Gubbins.

'Ah pigs,' replied Uncle, 'I got a bunch I'll sell you and wuth every penny I'll ask.'

'Don't want no pigs, George, I'm up to my eyes with pigs. I've got a nice litter of Spots I'll sell you.'

'Don't know as I want any more pigs, not pertickler like. I was hopin' to sell a few not buy a few,' rumbled Uncle.

'Well, never mind, they'll go. Pigs like that litter o' Spots won't take much sellin'.'

'Pig trade's slow, they tell me,' said Uncle.

'Always is at this time of year, but give it a wik or two, 'twill be different then. If nobody comes and takes a fancy to 'em, I'll try 'em in the market.'

'Trouble with the market, you never know what you'll get, one wik it's up an' so you send 'em the next an' trade's right down. Of course you can bring 'em home, but there's the expense, double journey, an' all for nothing. No, I allus like to sell at home, Harold. If I can, but as you know, you can't allus.'

'They're a wonderful lot.'

'I dare say, an' I'd take 'em off your hands if I could see me way clear, an' the price was right.'

'Oh, the price is right. I'm a reasonable man.'

'Of course you be, an' I be, I'm a reasonable man meself. You an' me, Harold, we be the sort as can do business. But just now – well you know what 'tis like, an' I know how I be fixed. A fair few pigs around me, an' all on 'em yuttin' thur heads off. But – well – as I'm here – 'twould be no harm in lookin' at 'em.'

'No harm at all, George, no harm at all.'

We went and had a look at the calves, at the horses in the

stable, at the cows, a yard of bullocks, a stack of hay. Uncle George waxed enthusiastic about calves, horses, cows, bullocks and hay. We came to the pigs, uncharacteristically Uncle showed less than his usual enthusiasm for pigs. 'Allus got yer hand in yer pocket with pigs,' he muttered as we passed from one pen of pigs to another.

'The litter of Spots I was tellin' you about are over there,' said Mr Gubbins.

'Oh ah,' rumbled Uncle George, 'let's have a look at 'em.'

We inspected the Spots. 'Eight hogs and four hilts,' said Mr Gubbins. 'Ain't they a picture, a good level lot.'

'They're not a bad bunch,' admitted Uncle rather grudgingly. 'Their mother's out in the paddock, just gone to my Gloucester boar again,' said Mr Gubbins.

'If they had some powders . . .' began Uncle.

'They've had some,' said Mr Gubbins.

'Wise,' rumbled Uncle George.

'All nicely healed, cut 'em meself, I allus do. In fact, I do a bit of castratin' for some, a bit of a sideline y'know,' said Mr Gubbins who then started to laugh.

'What be you laughin' about?' asked Uncle.

'There's an old woman, not far from here, well, she come to me t'other day an' said, "Oh, Mr Gubbins, it's my tom cat, I wonder if you'd doctor him for me." Well, she's a nice old woman an' as poor as a church mouse an' so I castrated her cat for nothing. "Oh thank you, Mr Gubbins," she said, "I'll do the same for you one day."'

We made our way slowly back to the baker's van. 'Nice bunch o' little pigs,' said Uncle. 'I don't want any more pigs pertickler like but just as a matter o' interest, what be you asking?'

'Nineteen bob a piece.'

'What!' exclaimed Uncle. 'And I allus thought you was a reasonable man.'

'I thought you were, George, but a reasonable man would know that was a reasonable price.'

'It's a dull time o' the year, Harold, pigs nor nothin's movin' much. Now if you was to say fourteen bob, that 'ould be reasonable an' realistic. Why, at that price or a bob less I might be tempted, although I don't want pigs pertickler at the moment.'

'You're a hard man, George.'

'It's hard times, Harold, a man can't afford to go chuckin' money about.'

'What'll you give, George? Make an offer, an' make it sensible.'

'When you said nineteen bob, you knocked me all of a quiver, Harold. I thought to myself, have Harold Gubbins gone clean out of his mind.'

'Well, what are they worth to you, George? They're a grand bunch of pigs and if you had the handlin' of 'em they'd soon be an even grander bunch.'

'There's summat in that, Harold, soak me bob if there ain't,' said Uncle George, at last showing an interest.

'You're a master chap with pigs, George, you've told me so yourself.'

'I'll give you fifteen bob,' said Uncle emphatically.

'Eighteen' retorted Mr Gubbins, now alert.

'Be you tryin' to rob me?'

'Rob you? I'm givin' 'em away.'

'Not a penny more.'

'A bob less, you can have 'em for a bob less as I've known you for a long time.'

'Sixteen,' said Uncle George slowly.

'Seventeen,' said Mr Gubbins quickly.

'Done!' said Uncle George loudly, and smack went the hand of Mr Gubbins on the hand of Uncle George.

Another mug of cider and then we left Mr Gubbins, but by then the light was fading. By the time we had delivered nearly all the remaining bread and been subjected to the hindrances of various customers, dusk had fallen. The last customer was a particular friend of Uncle's and by the time we left there it was quite dark and quite late.

We came within a quarter of a mile of our village, that is a quarter of a mile across the fields, but a mile and a half by road – and could see its lights twinkling. We also saw a light approaching us. The light came close to us and a voice cried, 'Stop!'

'Whoa' cried Uncle to the horse.

'It's you, George,' said the voice.

'Bob!'

'Bob I may be,' said the voice authoritatively, 'but I'm also Police Constable Blunt and you've got no lights.'

'Ain't I?' said Uncle George. 'Begod, you're right, I ain't.'

'It's an offence, no lights on the van at night.'

'They must 'ave gone out sudden like an' I never noticed,' said Uncle.

'You ain't got any lamps on your van to go out.'

'Ain't got no lamps, course I got lamps, allus have lamps. Somebody must 'ave stole 'em.'

'Did you ever have them on?'

'Allus 'ave 'em on, except when they're bein' cleaned an' filled. That's what it is, young Ron never put 'em back. An' I should have been home in the daylight if I hadn't been unaccountably delayed.'

'Drinking again, I suppose, you're not making it any better for yourself. Oh dear, George, this is most upsetting, I didn't want any more trouble, this being my last couple of weeks here.'

'Movin' are you?'

'Yes, kind of promotion y'know. Known for some time it was comin'.'

'Oh, I'm so pleased, but I knew it wouldn't be long, a keen officer of the law like you was bound to better hisself, the only wonder is it have took so long.'

'These lights, George.'

'Oh ah, I be gettin' down, hold the hoss's head, just got to pop behind the hedge. Could do it here in the road y'know as I'm in charge of a hoss. Got his head? – well, you're in charge now, so I s'pose I'd better go behind the hedge an' the boy here.'

Once we were over the stile and in the field Uncle whispered to me, 'Hush, boy, an' up along the footpath as hard an' as quiet as your legs'll take you. Go on now, don't hang about, it's time you were home abed.'

'What are you going to do, Uncle?'

'Hush, boy, hush, this is no time for talkin' an' dawdlin', I'm goin' home as fast as my legs'll take me, I be got tired an' I want to get to bed.'

'The horse, Uncle, the horse and the van,' I said, as we ran up the field.

'The hoss an' the van's all right, couldn't be in better hands, safe as houses. P.C. Blunt'll look after them.'

★ ★ ★ ★ ★

'And,' said Uncle George, when he came to dinner next day, 'I were in bed when Blunt arrived with the horse and van. It was almost an hour afore he come, he must have waited and held the horse for some time afore it tumbled to him as I wasn't coming back. I'm sorry in a way as I couldn't have stopped to have watched him, but 'twas gettin' late an' I was anxious to get to bed.'

'What did he say when he did arrive?' asked Father.

'Oh, he weren't very sweet, he shouted a bit an' cussed a bit. I looked at him outa me bedroom window and said 'twas a fine thing wakin' people up an' gettin' 'em out of bed. Somehow, that made him wusser; then he said, "Here's yer horse." And I said, "Unharness him and put him back in the stable; his grub's all ready, you wun't have ther work o' that." But he 'ouldn't, he just tied the horse up an' went off mutterin' an' cussin'. So I had to go down an' see to the hoss meself.'

'Do you think it was wise, doing a trick like that?' asked Father. 'Won't he have you for it?'

'You'll be in court again,' said Mother, 'and you won't get off so lightly this time.'

'No, I won't,' said Uncle George, 'I should have been mind, if me wits hadn't come to me aid, he'd have had me for havin' no lights, I must have clean forgot 'em. But, what of it, the horse knew his way home in the dark an' if folk couldn't see me they'd no business on the road. Leastways that's how I see it, but I dare say that muntle Blunt wouldn't be able to see it in that light. And he'd have had me if me mind and me legs hadn't been nimble.'

'But what's to stop him having you now?' asked Father.

'He daresn't, everybody, even them old magistrates 'ould laugh at him when the full story come out,' said Uncle George.

'It's time you were had,' muttered Mother, 'and he'll have you sooner or later.'

'No, he wun't, he's goin' in less than a fortnight,' replied Uncle.

'I reckon you've driven him away,' said Father.

'Poor man,' said Mother, 'always so nicely spoken.'

'He weren't last night, he fair let rip with some awful words. I only hope Mrs Peabody didn't hear him on her way back from the spinney. 'Twasn't fit for a woman's ears, 'twasn't fit for my ears or anybody's. I'm very surprised that an officer of the law should use such words, an' shoutin' 'em too. But I shan't hold it agen him, he were tired I expect. Bury the hatchet I allus say. I'll give him a jar o' me special afore he goes, a drop of that perry he's so fond on.'

'Drink!' screeched Mother, 'Drink, drink, nothing but drink, can you think of nothing but drink? Drink and disgrace, you'll drive me to drink before you've done.'

'I'll take him some o' me best bacon as well,' said Uncle George. 'Bob, old fellow, I'll say, let bygones be bygones, you're a man who does his duty an' I'm pleased you're off to do it somewhere else. There, what could be fairer than that?'

Chapter Seven
Two Men Went to Mow

Of course (said Uncle George) perry is dangerous stuff, it's sly y'see, 'specially new perry. It's very palatable and you be tempted to keep on drinkin' it, but you mustn't, but some do, as you know. There's all manner o' pears an' all manner o' perry. Barland's the best, why, the smell on't 'ull make you drink. There's Huffcap an' Merrylegs, Startle-Cock an' Steelyer Balls, Stinkin' Bishop an' Rumble-Jumble. And there's Blakeneys, that can scour you out if it comes from trees on rich ground – it ain't called the circus pear for nothin', new or old 'tis deadly stuff.

I can mind the time ol' Bill Buckle had a bet on an' the perry nearly did for him. You've never heard of Bill Buckle? I thought everyone had heard of Bill Buckle, still, I suppose you be too young to have heard of him, he bin dead an' gone many a year now I s'pose, 'tis a wonder how time do go. I wonder where it do go, there must be a great stack on it somewhere. Bill Buckle, poor ol' Bill Buckle, I ain't heard his name mentioned for a long time; nor I ain't give ol' Bill Buckle a thought since can't remember when. Master chap with a scythe, I must ask Reuben if he remembers him.

Who's Bill Buckle? Well, I'm tellin' you who he was if you'd only listen. He worked for Noakes' father an' his father afore him, reg'lar handy chap on a farm he were, turn his hand to most nearly everythin', milkin', ploughin', ditchin', hedgin', thatchin'. But what he most prided himself on was mowin' with a scythe, he could fair make a scythe sing when he got into his stride. Swish, swish, swish, from dawn to dusk. Of course, he knew how to put an edge on a scythe, that's the secret, a good edge what'll last. Wouldn't let anyone else touch his scythe, nor any of his other tools for that matter. Kept 'em to hisself, his axes, spades, saws, hoes, pikes, bill hooks an' hedge bills an' all. Somebody hid some of his tools one day, the ones he wanted to use pertickler, and off home he went, wouldn't do not more work that day. Some varmint have got me tools, he said, I can't work without me tools, I ain't accustomed to working with any old tools, I ain't used to it an' I ain't goin' to get used to it, I can't work, so 'tis no good stopin' here, I'm off it. Proud an' independent, y'see, an' such a good workman, Noakes or nobody dared say a word to him.

I knew another chap who was just the same about his tools, nobody else was allowed to have 'em, an' if anybody hid 'em just for devilment, off home he'd go. Some o' the old uns was like that, independent an' touchy. But none of 'em could swing a scythe like ol' Bill Buckle. There was only one thing wrong with him, he couldn't leave the cider alone. Lived in the village, next to Dan Teakle's, well it weren't Dan's then, 'twas his father's. Had a wife an' five kids, big strappin' 'oman his wife was, and Bill, he had a big bushy moustache, – I can see that big moustache of his – big, well-built chap he was. Good tempered chap, except over his tools, even when he'd had a drop too much he was still affable, different to a lot what do get ill-tempered when they've got the cider in 'em. All gone now, ol' Bill Buckle dead an' gone many a long year an' not a member of the fambly left around here. But there's still plenty who do remember ol' Bill, Dan Teakle for one, Noakes of course, an' Alf Tucker an' plenty more besides.

Now, how did I come to be talkin' about Bill Buckle? What made – oh, I remember – let me get me pipe goin' an' I'll tell ye.

'Twas on a summer evenin' in the Lion. Noakes' father said 'Bill Buckle's a master with a scythe, he can make some grass fall, there ain't a chap as can equal him with a scythe.'

'That's right,' said Dan Teakle's father, an' several others said the same. Most nearly all of 'em in the Lion agreed, except one or two what kept their mouths shut, an' Dick Watkins – he was the father of Watkins what lives up top o' the village. Dick, he fancied hisself with a scythe an' while Teakle an' Noakes an' t'others were singin' the praises o' Bill Buckle he just sat there lookin' glum.

That might ha' bin the end on't, an' I'd have had no story to tell ye if it hadn't been that Noakes an' Teakle an t'others hadn't gone on an' on 'bout what a master chap Buckle were with a scythe. 'There's none who could mow much more'n half that Bill could, not in the same time,' said one.

'Ho, yus there is,' said Dick Watkins, 'I could mow just as much in the same time, in fact, I could mow a sight more. Bill Buckle ain't the only chap what can handle a scythe.'

'Hold hard, Dick,' said one, 'You be good with a scythe, but you ain't as good as Bill.'

'Ain't as good as Bill,' growled Dick, and spat. 'I'm gooder than Bill any day of the wik.'

'You be good, but you baint as good,' said another.

'Ho, baint I just,' snorted Dick. 'I'd stake me life on't. I'd show y'all I was if only I had the chance.'

'I'd put my money on Bill,' said Noakes. 'I'd put five pun on him any time against you, Dick, or any other man.'

Dick just sat an' scowled, I could tell if anyone said much more about Bill being a better man with a scythe, Dick Watkins would turn very nasty. Suddenly Mr Teakle said, 'Why not have a contest to see which is the better man?'

'And Dick would soon show some of you,' piped up Joe Peglar, him bein' a pertickler friend of Dick's, an' no doubt hopin' to please Dick. But Dick didn't seem none too pleased by Teakle's idea, nor no more by Peglar's remark.

Others took up Teakle's idea. 'I've got a medder what would be just right for the job. Bill 'ould agree like a shot and I could fix up with Dick's boss – we could have the contest on Saturday,' said Noakes.

'Oh no,' growled Dick Watkins, 'That job ain't comin' off.'

'Why not?' says one an' another, 'atter all your talk, be you afeard Bill 'ould beat you?'

'No, I baint,' muttered Dick.

'Course he ain't,' chimed in Peglar.

'What's the matter then, Dick?' asked Mr Teakle.

'Bill would have an unfair advantage, 'twouldn't be right . . .' said Dick.

''Twouldn't be right,' put in Peglar.

'Why's that?' asked Teakle.

Joe Peglar looked blank and said nothing. Dick said, 'Bill'd be mowin' on familiar ground an' I'd be on strange ground.'

'That's easily settled,' said Harry Abbot. 'I've got a little medder all nice an' level an' with grass just fit for mowin' – Bill an' Dick can have their contest there. Next Saturday would be just about right.'

'That's more like it!' exclaimed Joe Peglar, 'ain't it Dick?' Dick didn't seem as pleased about it as Joe did, he didn't look none too pleased with Joe neither, although Joe was a petickler mate of his.

'That's it,' said several. 'That's on,' said t'others. 'I'll put five pun on Bill,' said Noakes, 'damned if I don't.'

'I'll put two bob on Dick,' said Pegler, 'yus, I will, an' I'd put more if I had it.'

'Five pun on Bill, two bob on Dick, that's about the size on't,' I said, although I was only a bit of a boy chap at the time and had only just started goin' to the Lion. Dick didn't like that either, that an' the talk about Bill's prowess an' the idea of a contest had rattled him.

'Saturday's payday, so I'll be able to put a bit more on you than I thought, Dick,' said Pegler.

Anyway, to cut a long story short, 'twas all fixed up. Two one acre an' a bit pieces was all paced out an' marked down in Harry Abbot's little medder just out o' the village an' away from anywhere – nice little medder, all flat, ideal for the job, an' the grass were just right too. They marked it out on the Friday evening, Abbot an' Noakes an' Teakle an' Percy Ludgater from the Lion – there weren't much goin' on but what Percy had to have a hand in it. An' Bill Buckle an' Dick Watkins, an' Dick's boss – he went along he said to see fair play, he weren't goin' to have his men made a fool on. Joe Peglar, he were there an' a few others, an' I went, although I was only a boy chap at the time.

They started mowin' on the Saturday, almost at peep o' day. Oh, there was great excitement about the job, it was the talk o' the Lion the night before. Did I tell you Mr Teakle was takin' bets on it? No, well he were. At first it were even money on the two of 'em, but that job weren't any bottle, Teakle would have lost money on that, there weren't many takers for Dick to win, not at even money. So Teakle had to offer two to one; a bob on Dick an' if he won you'd have two bob winnings and your own bob back. Support for Dick picked up a bit, but it didn't satisfy some, they wanted better odds on Dick; Joe Peglar he wanted four to one, although he was such a supporter of Dick.

Anyway, as I've said, they started early on the Saturday morning. I went over to see 'em start. Noakes an' Dick's boss were there, and Teakle of course an' a few others. Bill an' Dick offed with thur jackets an' started to whet their scythes, givin' 'em long strokes with the rubbers. Percy Ludgater came while they was doin' it.

Noakes looked at his watch, Dick's boss looked at his watch, Teakle looked at his'n, Percy Ludgater looked at his'n – and made a show on't too. I daresay Joe Peglar 'ould have done the same if he'd had one to look at. I couldn't quite see the sense on't meself, if they was goin' to start together, what odds was the time?

'Time to start, men,' shouted Percy Ludgater, who seemed to have appointed hisself referee or summat. 'And may the best man win.'

'Hear, hear,' shouted Joe Peglar.

'And may the best man win,' repeated Percy Ludgater, giving Joe a nasty look.

I couldn't see the point of Percy sayin' that, not unless he knew summat the rest of us didn't know. Of course the best man would win, that was what it was about, that was why they was havin' the contest. And most on us already knew who the best man was – it was only Dick's boastin' ways what had brought it all on – Bill Buckle would win hands down.

Each man went to his appointed patch o' grass, about one and a half acres, or maybe a bit more for the each on 'em. Bill, tall an' big with it; Dick, short an' stocky, each with his scythe.

Swish, swish, swish, went their scythes into the dew laden grass, with the sun peepin' shyly down on 'em. High above a skylark sang in the delicate air of that newly born day in June. But the skylark's song made no sweeter sound than the song of those swinging scythes. Swish, swish, swish.

We watched 'em, Noakes, Dick's boss, Teakle, Ludgater, me an' t'others, not one on us said a word for a while. Both of the mowers worked with a will, back an' forth went their scythes. Long, swinging, firm but gentle strokes, the scythes became part o' the men, the men part of the scythes. I couldn't stop there all mornin' an' neither could most of t'others. As we left, Noakes said, 'They be goin' at it neck an' neck, but when the sun's well up Watkins will start to lag, while Bill will still be goin' the same pace.'

'Stick to it, men,' shouted Percy Ludgater. 'We'll be back later.' Percy he was talkin' very big as we walked back to the village, you'd have thought it was his contest an' his medder.

'Nobody would take my five pun,' said Noakes as we parted. 'You can't blame 'em 'cos it would have bin certain profit for me.'

Later on when I returned, Bill Buckle was well ahead, as most of us expected, he'd finish his patch long afore Dick Watkins, that was plain for all to see. Swish, swish, went his blade, sweet like, although the sun was gettin' in the grass. Dick, give him his due, was goin' at it like a good un, but he must have known 'twere all up with him.

Joe Peglar came back, he went over to Dick and then to Bill, back to Dick, over to Bill, hoppin' about like a gadfly.

Bill Buckle only had one complaint, he'd downed all the cider in his costrel [small hand barrel holding about four pints] and was feelin' dry. Peglar went off to report this to Dick, hopin' no doubt it would bring him some comfort. I told Bill I'd bring him a drop when I came back later in the afternoon and then off I went again to do a bit in the shop.

When I went down to the medder again, Bill wasn't as forrard as I thought he 'ould be. Not as that meant much, Buckle's a good natured chap – which is more than could be said for Watkins. And so, I thought to meself, Bill have steadied up a bit in order not to show Watkins up too much. Not as I'd have done such a thing, not after the way Watkins had bin boastin' in the Lion.

Just then Bill laid down his scythe an' walked off an' went behind the hedge. Not as that meant anythin', a man can't mow all day without goin' behind the hedge some time. And I said as much when someone remarked, 'He've gone behind the hedge.'

'What of it?' I said. 'It ain't the fust time,' I was told by one an' another. 'He's at it all the time.'

Back Bill came, bucklin' that gurt belt he allus wore, an' soak me bob, it weren't long afore he were off behind the hedge again.

'It's that perry he bin gettin' down him,' said one on 'em who'd bin there all the afternoon.

Damn my rags, he'd hardly got back in his stride and off he ran at a jog-trot, unbucklin' his belt as he went towards the hedge.

'It's that perry what Joe Peglar brought him,' I was told. He ought to have left it alone I said. 'Of course he ought, but you know what Bill's like an' I reckon mowin' ding-dong all day in this sun's thirsty work.'

'He's goin' ding-dong all the time behind the hedge,' I said, 'an' while he's at that caper, downin' an' uppin' his trousers an' fiddlin' with that gurt belt, Dick Watkins is catchin' up on him. A few more trips an' ding-dongin' an downin' an' uppin' an' all an' Watkins will be ahead of him. Besides, all that traipsin' about will take the strength clean out of him, an' I'll lose me five bob.'

'I stand to make a profit out of this,' said Teakle, 'if Bill loses as he's bound to at this rate, but I'd still rather see him win, he's the better man.'

'He ain't the better man now,' I said, 'it was a dirty trick, I reckon Dick Watkins put Peglar up to't when he saw Bill forgin' ahead. But it was foolish of Bill.'

'I'm tellin' you, George, I don't like it,' said Teakle.

'Damn foolish,' I said. I couldn't stop there to watch it, the humiliation of Buckle, the crowin' of Watkins, an' the loss of my half-crown. Besides, I had work to do at the shop.

At night I went to the Lion. I thought to meself I've lost half a crown today, I might as well swallow another an' try an' forget the fust. Mind, I had a good mind not to go; Watkins 'ould be there crowin' an' that Peglar. But if they were I'd tell 'em what I thought of 'em. A damn dirty trick – after all these years I still don't like talkin' about it, disgustin', disgraceful, dirty. Teakle an' Noakes an' some of t'others would tell 'em too. Ludgater, if he had anythin' about him would disqualify Watkins, after all Ludgater had appointed hisself umpire an' if he took the job on he should be man enough to carry it out. I reckoned, one way an' t'other, there'd be a fair ol' barney at the Lion afore the night was out.

'Beat him all ends up,' Noakes told me. 'Into a cocked hat,' said another. 'Left him standing,' said somebody. 'Why ain't he in here then? I was sure he'd be in here a crowin',' I said.

'Bill Buckle ain't the sort to crow,' said Ludgater. 'He ain't got much to crow about,' I said.

'He's a master mower,' said one.

'Ah, he's a master chap with a scythe,' I said, 'and he's a master chap with the jar, an' as he's shown today he's a master chap runnin' behind the hedge. Oh, ah, he's a master all right.'

'That's no matter,' said one. 'It is, it's a disgrace, disgustin',' I said. 'Let bygones be bygones,' said another. 'I will,' I said, 'when they've gone by a little more.'

'But he won,' said Percy Ludgater.

'Won, be damned,' I said. 'How could Buckle win? He was too busy gettin' behind that hedge.'

'He soon stopped that, when he saw he was gettin' behind,' somebody said.

'He was gettin' behind all right, gettin' his behind behind that hedge.'

'But he stopped that,' said one.

'Stopped it? Why, when a man starts that caper he can't stop, 'tis out of his control,' I said. 'So how could he have won?'

'He just took his trousers off an' kept on a mowin' an' a goin',' said Noakes.

So there you are, boy, that's the story of the mowin' contest in Harry Abbot's medder what's now called Bill's medder. I told you Bill Buckle were a master of a chap.

Chapter Eight

Adventures with a Motor Bike

Nobody taught me to ride a bike (said Uncle George) I didn't have no lessons nor nothin' like that, I taught meself, I just got on and off I went.

The chap brought the motor bike on a Sunday evenin' one summer. Atter a bit o' talk, he started the engine and told me to sit on the bike to get the feel on him an' to see how I liked meself on him. So I got on an' started to get the feel on him an' got to like meself on him. Then he started to tell me about the controls, all manner of them, but I weren't takin' it all in, I were too busy gettin' the feel of him still. I'd never been on one afore an' it takes a bit o' time an' concentration to get the feel of a motor bike if you ain't never bin astride one afore.

Then – afore I knew where I was, I was gone – I was off – I must ha' touched summat what made him go. And off I went, not very fast, but too fast for the fella what had brought him. He started runnin' an' shoutin', but he weren't nimble enough, and I had other things to think about to be able to take any notice of what he were shoutin'. Besides, there was the noise of the motor bike an' the chap was out of breath an' couldn't shout, not to make a job on't.

'Whoa! whoa!' I shouted, but of course, that weren't no good. I didn't know what to do anyway, 'twere a full-time job keepin' meself on the thing. An' mind I got as I didn't like meself on't either. I didn't dare touch any of those controls, not knowin' what they was for. I'd touched one an' look what had happened, I wasn't goin' to risk another. I might go faster if I did – an' I was goin' fast enough as 'twas. Anythin' might happen if I meddled, enough an' more'n enough had happened already.

This is goin' to be the end of you, George me lad, I thought to meself. A promisin' young chap's goin' to meet 'is

Waterloo. If you don't kill yourself, at least you'll end up in the infirmary, broken bones an' splints an' bandages, probably a cripple for life. It didn't look none too promisin' an' there I was goin', an' goin' I knew not where. But as I went, I was gettin' the feel o' that bike, oh, I got the feel of'n right enough an' I stuck to him, I wasn't goin' to fall off if I could help it.

Mind you, I was doin' more than just holdin' tight. As I was goin' me wits was workin'. There's only one thing for't, I thought to meself, hold on an' go careful, sooner or later we're bound to run out of petrol. Of course, I didn't know if 'twould be sooner or later, I hoped it would be sooner, but feared 'twould be later. If 'twere sooner 'twouldn't be too bad, but I'd have to go careful in case 'twas later. Keep doublin' round as much as I could otherwise I could end up miles from home.

So I just sat on there holdin' tight an' hopin' the petrol 'ould soon give out. There wasn't the traffic about in those days and I had the road all to meself, an' along it I chugged, not very fast, but fast enough for me. I went round a corner an' then some distance ahead I saw three chaps walkin' along.

As I got close to 'em I started to shout. They all turned an' looked at me. I shouted an' told 'em what had happened an' then I gave 'em instructions. 'Get ready,' I said, 'an' when I come up alongside, grab hold o' the bike. Grab hold an' hold hard.' I came up almost alongside 'em. 'Right chaps,' I shouted, 'grab hold!'

And they came like terriers at a rat. And they pounced like cats at a mouse. An' they held on like limpets. An' I came to a stop like a rabbit in a net.

One of the chaps put his hand out an' did summat. 'Why didn't you do that?' he asked. 'If I'd known as much as I do now, I should ha' done that,' I said.

They were damn good chaps, they didn't mess about, when I gave the word, they collared that bike like a shot an' pulled me to a halt. Mark you, it made 'em scuff their fit fairish, it made 'em puff an' blow, but they did it. Rajah rhubarb, they did it. I gave 'em all the loose change I'd got in me pocket. That were cheaper than a hospital job, I'll warrant. No broken bones; saved me from bein' a cripple for the rest of me life. They were damn good chaps, I was lucky to drop on chaps like it. I told 'em they were damn good chaps. But it was me nimble wits what really saved me. That, an' me gettin' the feel of the bike so soon. Come to think of it, I'd mastered that bike by the time them chaps got hold of me, if they hadn't happened to be about, I dare say I should ha' coped. As I allus say, you can't get a good chap down.

And that, me boy, is how I learnt to ride a motor bike, no help or instruction from anybody. I just got on the bagger an' away to go.

★   ★   ★   ★   ★

By and by (said Uncle George) I bought a sidecar for my motor bike. It took a lot of gettin' used to, it was all right on the straight, but on the corners it was the very devil until I got in the way on't. Mind, it didn't take me long to master it, but it was a painful time while I was learnin' the way. I had a few nasty spills an' tumbles.

There was the time I landed in the hedge, that shook me up no end and I got a gurt thorn in me hand. I called in at Aggie's later that night, a cold ol' night it were too, I call to mind.

'What's the matter, George?' Aggie asked. 'You seem in a bit of a state.'

And who, I told her, wouldn't be in a state ater being flung sky high an' then landin' flump in a hedge an' gettin' a gurt thorn in his hand.

Ol' Sam asked if it were a blackthorn, an' I told him I didn't know what kind of a thorn it was, it had gone in that deep.

'Let me see, let me see,' says our Aggie. 'Let me have a look and see if I can get it out.'

'Let it bide where 'tis,' I said, 'an' kip warm.'

'Oh, oh,' says Aggie, 'you ought to let me get it out.'

'If 'tis a blackthorn,' says Sam, 'it'll kill you. If it's a quickthorn it wun't be so bad. But if it's a blackthorn it'll be fatal. They'm terrible poisonous, blackthorns be. I dare say it's too late now, the poison an' all is doin' its work already. If you'd got it out straight away an' bathed your hand an' used some iodine immediately, there might have bin a chance.'

'Oh, oh,' our Aggie cried, 'let me get it out, let me get the iodine.'

''Twould be a waste of time now,' said that ol' Sam.

'Get off to the doctor as fast as you can, George,' cried our Aggie, lookin' very upset an' wringin' her hands.

'It'll be all right,' I told her, 'I'll bathe me hand when I get home, I'll douse me hand with iodine and I'll swallow some stuff I got by me. Anyway, I've got a powerful constitution, an ol' thorn wun't do me much harm, let'n bide an' kip warm, an' stop fussin'.'

'Well, have a nice cup o' tea, and an aspirin,' says Aggie.

'You'll be a jud un afore you know where you are, you see if you ain't, an' when you be you'll see I was right,' says ol' Sam. And for once in his life, ol' Sam were nearly right. I had a terrible bad hand and a terrible time on't, it turned septic somethin' cruel. I was down at the doctor's an' when I wasn't down at the doctor's, the nurse was up at my place dressin' it an' all.

'You was lucky,' ol' Sam said, after it had cleared up. 'Lucky be damned,' I said, there wasn't nothin' lucky about bein' in mortal pain an' sufferin' all the hours of the day an' night with never a wink o' sleep an' very near a jud un. Of course, I were lucky in a way, havin' a powerful constitution, if I hadn't I reckon it would have been napoo, that thorn would have put the kybosh on me.

And I thought ol' Colonel were a goner too, through that ol' motor bike an' sidecar while I was still gettin' the hang of it. In fact, I'd pretty well mastered it by the time of the incident with Colonel. I'd taken him out for a bit of a ride an' I'd got the feel on't pretty well, so when we come to a straight bit I let the ol' bike have it, I let rip, just to let Colonel know as I could handle the tack. 'Steady, George, steady,' Colonel kept shoutin'. 'Don't you fear none,' I said, 'I know what I'm doin'.'

'But,' said Colonel, 'I know this road better'n you do, there's a sharpish corner just before we get to that village over there.' Well, I knowed that, but what I didn't realise was that the corner was goin' to come on us so soon, but it would 'ave bin all right, if only Colonel hadn't distracted me attention with all his shoutin' an' wavin' his arms about.

Anyway, the long an' the short of it was, we hit the verge an' flumped down into a hole an' poor ol' Colonel was pitchy-poled out an' shot into the ditch. It would never have 'appened if only he'd behaved hisself, it was all his own fault; shoutin' an' wavin' his arms an' jaggin' about. A deep ol' ditch it was an' there was poor ol' Colonel at the bottom of it, as still as a log, as quiet as a mouse, he never as much as twitched, if he'd been pole-axed he couldn't 'ave made a better job on't.

One an' another come rushin' up to see what had happened; soon there was quite a little crown gawpin' down into the ditch at poor ol' Colonel.

'Fetch a doctor,' from one. 'Fetch an ambulance,' from another. 'Fetch a policeman,' somebody said. 'Fetch a spade,' I said, 'an' cover'n up, 'cos he's a jud un.'

★ ★ ★ ★ ★

It was (continued Uncle George, a little while later) a long time before old Colonel came out with me on the bike again. In fact, it was a few days afore he as much as spoke to me. 'Let bygones be bygones,' I told him, 'I took you out, you had a nice ride and a good day, and you enjoyed yourself apart from that little job. You had a little tumble, but you ain't none the wuss for it, so you ain't got nothin' to grumble about, bury the hatchet.'

But, I must admit, I had some funny experiences with that motor bike an' sidecar.

I took your father to town one Saturday night – it was long afore he was married – we went to the Hippodrome – they had live performances there then; comedians an' singers – oh, they had some wonderful singers, couldn't some of them girls sing an' not much on 'em either, but some on 'em could sing like nightingales – jugglers, damn my rags, some of them fellas were clever – acrobats, those girls had even less on than the singers.

Now, where was I, what was I tellin' you? – Oh, yes, when I took your father to the Hippodrome or rather when we was comin' back home. Everything was all right until we got about halfway back an' then your father started actin' in a most peculiar manner. I didn't know what to make of him, his behaviour had me flummoxed. I'd never seen the like of what he was doin'. Rajah rhubarb, I'd seen some antics by one an' another, but never nothin' like them antics your father was at. There he was, jerkin' his head like one o'clock an' as reg'lar as clockwork. Not just ord'nary jerkin' but real fierce, vicious jerkin', a proper performance o' real high steppin' jerkin', the like of which I'd never sin before an' never want to see no more.

If it had been ord'nary jerkin' I wouldn't have minded, I should have thought he'd most likely got a bit over excited by

the sight of them scantily dressed females at the Hippodrome
– some chaps get that way by them sort o' sights y'know,
'specially them as a'nt got the constitution for't. But this was
no ord'nary jerkin', this was jerkin' in some order.

It disturbed me; over his head would lunge towards me.
Perhaps he'd got a bit of a spasm, I thought, and it'll pass
over, I'll kip me mouth shut, I thought – best to kip goin' an'
say nothin'– the sooner he's home, the better. But he didn't
get better, he got wusser, it seemed he'd taken a proper likin'
to the job. He were a rarin' an' jerkin' an' a jumpin' like
billy-o. Fair rockin' the sidecar with his capers.

'Pon me soul, I thought to meself, me brother's gone a
wrong un. He ain't a right un, he's a proper wrong un an' no
mistake. Better get him home as quick as I can, I thought,
afore he gets any wusser as he's already gettin' wusser every
minute. I let the ol' bike have it, I let rip, I fair tore along that
road. An' as for me brother who'd gone a wrong un, he was
lettin' rip in some order, his head were bobbin' an' jerkin' an'
lungin' nineteen to the dozen. 'Hey, steady on,' I shouted, but
he was past all understandin' an' reason. It wouldn't have
surprised me if his yud had snapped right off his shoulders,
the way he was goin' at it.

Whatever would they say when I got him back, that was if I
ever got him back all in one piece. He were too far gone for the
doctor to cope with him, he was a proper wrong un an' no
mistake. It would be the asylum for him an' they'd have their
hands full with a chap with his antics.

His wits had gone, an' I was at my wits end, there was
nothing for't but to go as hard as I could an' get the poor
fellow home. An' he was going' at it as hard as ever he could,
his yud was goin' at it like a woodpecker at a tree, but wusser.

He's bound to tire, I thought, even if he is a wrong un, he
can't kip that caper goin' much longer. But, damn my rags, he
could an' he did, his constitution must have been summat
wonderful to kip that job a goin' like he did, even if he had
gone a wrong un.

There'll be no more shows for you m'lad, I said to meself,
you're a proper show yerself. No more acrobats an' jugglers,
you're doin' enough acrobatin' an' jugglin' with that poor ol'
yud of your'n to last a lifetime. No, there'll be no more
Hippodrome an' scantily dressed females for you, it'll be a
padded cell an' men in white coats for you, m'lad. Oh, dear,

oh dear, it's a sad case, cut off in yer prime, an' you, me only brother.

What in the world could have brought these capers on, I wondered. We'd seen a fair lot o' bare legs an' arms an a bit of bosom too, an' had a pint of beer. But bare legs an' arms an' a bit of bosom would never cause this. My brother must have had a bit of weakness in the head what we had never noticed an' it had now taken hold an' was fair lettin' go, really lettin' rip. It was a pitiful sight, it fair broke me heart to see'n goin' at it.

It's unaccountable, I said to meself. It was so bad, I tried to avoid seein' his capers, but damn me rags, you can't ignore that sort o' thing when it's goin' on right beside you. The only thing I could think all the rest of the way home was, 'My brother's gone a wrong un.'

When we got to the village I slowed down. My brother slowed down. He-up, I thought to meself, that's a good sign, p'rhaps he's goin' off it at last. But he was still jerkin' an' joggin' an' jaggin', only it wasn't so fast. Mebbe if he takes things quietly and nothin' upsets him, after a while, he'll give the whole job up. But he were still at it, the way he lunged towards me, 'twas a wonder he didn't knock his brains out, such as they were. He'd gone a wrong un, I was convinced o' that, an' so quickly too. One minute he was as right as rain an' then with no warnin' he'd gone a wrong 'un.

Thank King Peter, it was late when we got back to the village – there didn't seem to be anyone about. I didn't want it all over the place that me brother'd gone a wrong un; so I said to him, 'This is the kinda thing you want to kip to yerself. Try the best you can, let's see if you can keep it dark; your sort o' capers ain't the sort o' thing we want every Tom, Dick an' Harry to know about.' But he was past reason an' went on in the manner to which he'd got accustomed, a proper habit it was, 'cept it weren't proper, not to my way o' thinkin', nor wouldn't 'ave bin to any right thinkin' man – an' very few wrong thinkin' uns I should imagine.

We drew up in the yard in front of the house an' I stopped the bike. I took me time goin' round to'n, I thought this job an' the manner of handlin' him needs a bit of caution.

'Pon my soul, I'd had some shocks that night an' no mistake an' now I had another bagger!

When I got round to 'im, there he was standin' up an' as right as ninepence. He was tremblin' a bit – and who wouldn't after a performance like that – but not as you'd notice. Well, I looked at him an' he looked at me and I looked at him again – I'd had the stuffin' knocked out o' me, an' then I spoke to 'im.

'Whatever's bin the matter with you?' I asked. 'All them antics an' suchlike, all that head jerkin', jiggin' an' jaggin'. Those sort o' capers ain't no good to you nor nobody.'

'I've had a fair old time of it, George,' he said. 'And you bain't the only one,' I told him.

'It wasn't no joke,' he said. 'No, it wasn't,' I said, 'so why did you do't?'

'Do it,' he said, 'and what would you do if every second a damn great thing came an' thumped you on the head.'

Oh dear, I thought, he've stopped the jerkin' an' all, but he still ain't a right un', I'd better humour him. 'Come on,' I said to him, 'come on in an' get to bed, perhaps you'll feel better after a good night's sleep.'

'Sleep,' he said, 'I shan't get a wink of sleep until I've found out what it was.'

'It'll be gone now,' I said, just to humour him.

'Gone be baggered,' he said, 'Let's have a look round the sidecar an' see what 'tis, it ain't the sort o' thing that goes like that.'

No, I thought, an' your thing ain't the sort what's goin' to go all that easily. But to humour him I let him get on with it. I even struck a match so's he could have a better look.

'There 'tis,' he shouted, 'that's the bagger what have bin pesterin' me.'

Just to humour him I bent down an' had a look at the wheel of the sidecar. I saw somethin' like a balloon; it was part of the inner tube pokin' out from the tyre. 'It was bigger than that when it came round at me,' my brother said, 'I expect my weight squeezed it out more.'

And I said, 'Thank the Lord, you bain't a wrong un.'

*   *   *   *   *

I had another funny experience (said Uncle George) comin' back from the Hippodrome with the bike an' sidecar. No, it was the Palace, not the Hippodrome. I'd been to see *The Quaker Girl* with the schoolmaster. It was his idea, he was mad to go. '*The Quaker Girl*'s coming to the Palace, George,' he said, 'we must go and see that.' Oh, he was all afire about it.

'*The Quaker Girl*,' he kept saying, 'we mustn't miss that.' The week before it was on, he could talk 'bout nothing else when I saw him. He'd even started singing, 'Tell me pretty maiden, Are there any more at home like you?'

'It was all the rage in London, he said, 'and now we've the chance to see it.' According to him, it was proper, high class, professional performers coming and something not to be missed. Oh he was all afire wi' it, every time I saw him he kept on about it and at last he over-persuaded me. 'Righto,' I said, 'we'll go,' – mind I was quite keen to go meself, but there was no need to get over excited about it.

'Right,' he said, 'next Friday night. I'll book the seats.'

He got some good seats an' it was a good show. On the way out of the theatre, I lost Henry – Henry Dark, that was his name. I looked an' looked, but I couldn't see hide nor hair of him. Well, I thought, perhaps the nogman's out in the street, perhaps he's pushed on – there was a bit of a crush – a bit uncivil of him, bein' as I'd been good enough to take him an' all. But he wasn't out in the street either, I looked up an' down, but there was no sign of him.

Well, I thought, if he don't turn up in a minute or two, I'm off it an' he'll have to walk home an' serve'n right too, rushin' off in that uncivil manner. Then he come hurryin' out of the theatre. 'Where you bin?' I asked.

'I stopped to get some toffee,' he said.

We got to the motor bike an' set off. He was as jovial as could be, singin': 'A bachelor gay am I, though I've suffered from Cupid's dart.' He kep' up the singing for a mile or two and then he went silent. After a while I spoke to him, an' gettin' no answer I spoke to him again, louder this time. No answer. I left him alone for a bit an' then I had another try – damned uncivil of him I thought, after I'd bin good enough to take him out, but I thought I'd give 'im another chance. But still he didn't answer, he just sat there in the sidecar, my sidecar, like a deaf mute. Never as much acknowledged me, damned ignorant, I never thought anybody, 'specially a schoolmaster, could be so ignorant.

Oh, I thought to meself, you've turned a surly un an' no mistake, it'll be many a long day afore I take you out again, you ignorant bagger. A bachelor gay indeed, you're a sullen bagger, soak me bob if you ain't.

Another couple o' miles an' not a word out o' him, but I

ain't one to hold malice. P'rhaps he's been thinkin' or
summat, or p'rhaps he'd had his fad out an' would be ready to
be civil. Let bygones be bygones I said to meself an' spoke to
him loudly an' very affably too, which was uncommonly civil
of me, considerin' his behaviour.

But again, an' despite my kindness, an' civility, an' affabil-
ity, the bagger never uttered a word. It took my breath away,
it astounded me, I was flabbergasted. Never in all me born
days had I witnessed such unwarranted, downright ignorance.
An' him a schoolmaster, supposed to be an eddycated man, a
man teachin' children. He weren't fit to be in charge of a
donkey, the ill-bred varmint. I'd make it my business to have
a word with the parson about this – to think that such an
ignorant varmint was in charge o' children. I'd soon odds that,
damn my rags if I 'ouldn't.

Well, I thought, no more Palace, nor Quakers Girls for you,
Dark, you varmint, an' precious little more schoolmasterin'
for you, atter I've exposed you for the low, ill-bred, bad
natured ignorant fellow you be.

Yet, I didn't want to be too hard on him, so I gave him
another chance. I spoke to him again, just as though nothing
had happened. As a matter o' fact, nothing had happened, that
was the trouble, but you expect a chap to act civil, 'specially
after you've bin good to him. But no, I gave him chance again
an' again, an' never a word from him. You've gone a surly 'un,
I said to meself, I wonder what's got into you.

After another mile, an' nurn a squeak from him, I said,
'You be a surly sullen un.'

We came to the Green Man, an' I said, 'We'll go in an' have
a drink.' Still never a word from him, an' I said, 'Please
yerself, I'm goin' in to have a drink, you can stop out here an'
sulk or do what you like. I'm goin' to take me time, I hope you
be frozen stiff when I come out' – it was a sharpish ol' night –
'it ain't no odds to me nor nobody, the way you be nobody'll
notice.'

When we stopped, he jumped out like one o'clock an'
rushed into the Green Man without utterin' a word. Ho, I
thought, if you think I'm goin' to buy you a drink, you be
mistaken, you bagger.

He was nowhere to be seen when I got into the bar, not that
that worried me perticklar, I didn't want any more truck with
a chap who behaved in such a peculiar manner. The ungrate-

ful bagger could vanish never more to be seen for all as I cared. Then he come in, as nice as ninepence, an' said, 'Have another, George.'

'You're a nice 'un,' I said, 'whatever was the matter with you? All the way back you was as sullen an' as surly, then you rushed in here somewhere as though the devil was atter you. You be a nice 'un, indeed you be. I take you to the Palace put meself out pertickler to do't an' then you turn surly. All as I can say is, you be a nice un.'

'It was that toffee,' he said.

'Toffee be baggered. I ain't talkin' 'bout toffee, I'm talkin' 'bout ignorance, surliness an' ingratitude. A man in your position an' with your eddycation . . .'

'I broke a big piece off and put it in my mouth and started chewing it and my teeth got stuck – I couldn't speak . . .'

★ ★ ★ ★ ★

That's the trouble with some, they can't go anywhere but what they've got to be chompin' an' munchin' on the way home (continued Uncle George). I took Colonel into town one afternoon in the sidecar. Colonel muddled about here an' there, an' by the time we was ready to go home it was dark. Then just when we was about to go, he suddenly remembered he wanted some chitt'lings. He had to have 'em, he was desperate for 'em, he knew the very place where he could get 'em, he wouldn't be five minutes. And without as much as a 'by your leave', he scampered off.

Back he came as pleased as punch with the chitt'lings. 'You ready now?' I said, ''cos I hope you are, but whether you are or not, I'm goin'.'

We hadn't gone more'n a couple o' miles before he started on 'em. Gutsy ol' varmint, Colonel, couldn't kip his hands off 'em. After a while, he said, 'George, these chitt'lings ain't half good, they'm stuffed. You try some.'

He handed me some an' I put me tith into 'em an' said, 'Stuffed be damned, 'tis shit begod! They ain't bin cleaned.'

And then there was the time Reuben and I went off for the day with the motor bike. We got lost in the dark an' ol' Reuben was climbin' signposts an' strikin' matches to see the way.

An' we ran out of petrol an' had to sleep the night in a barn. Reuben complained that he was cold. There was a lot of ol' thatchin' pegs in the barn, so I chucked 'em over him an' said, 'See if they'll kip you warm,' but, d'you know, he didn't appreciate me kindly gesture.

An' at our show one year, it was a big affair in those days, flowers an' vegetables, swings an' roundabouts, an' trottin' races . . . Nearly everyone got drunk that year, including the parson an' the policeman. The poor ol' parson, – no, not Mr Bence, the one afore him – was frightened to go home an' face his missus. 'Take me for a spin in your sidecar, George,' he says, 'I need a bit of fresh air.' Fresh air be damned, he were as drunk as a lord, couldn't hardly stand. I was drivin' about most of the night with him. 'Hallelujah,' he kep' shoutin'. After a couple o' hours o' that caper, I'd had me fad out o' tourin' round an' about, but not him. 'It's a lovely night, George,' he says. 'It's a pity to go home yet.' Eventually he fell asleep, so I took'n back to the vicarage an' dumped him in the porch. 'May the Lord be with you,' I said, 'an' may the Lord protect you.'

Jack Perkins was another I had to take for a midnight ride. Poor ol' Jack was in all manner o' trouble, he had to get away an' without anyone knowin' he was goin' either. So I got'n away between two days. I met 'im at midnight with me motor bike and sidecar and I drove him into town an' put him on the train. Poor devil hadn't got hardly a bob in the world, just a suitcase with a few belongings. So before we parted I put me hand in me pocket an' brought out some notes – twenty-five quid it were. 'Here you are, Jack,' I said, 'this will keep you goin' for a bit.' The poor devil looked at it, there were tears in his eyes, an' said, 'I can't take all that, George.' Mind, it were a fair bit o' money in them days. An' I said, 'I ain't got no pertickler use for't at the moment, an' you have, an' if you don't take it I shall be most offended.' I ain't never sin Jack from that day to this, nor me twenty-five quid an' it were a long time ago, but I still ain't sorry I gave it to him.

Chapter Nine

A Beau and a Belle in a Belfry

Mrs Peabody came into the baker's shop. Her spectacles flashed and behind them a faint glint could be discerned in her eyes. Her thin lips were tight, she looked, as indeed she was, prim and smug; not at all the kind of woman to have secret assignations in the spinney with a man. But, as Uncle George said, still waters run deep, although nobody as far as I knew had any definite evidence of these still waters running deep in the way so often suggested by Uncle George. Mother was adamant that 'it was all a pack of lies'. Father took the view that it was 'bound to be right if our George says so.' Opinion was divided upon the subject, and with the exception of Uncle George, most of the villagers' discussion was muted.

Mrs Peabody was the church organist, she was a woman full of religion, but devoid of charity, a prominent member of the Mothers' Union and the Women's Institute. The leader of a small coterie which included Mrs Hatch the newsagent, Mrs Gerrish the postmaster's wife and Mother. Mrs Peabody was righteous; ever alive to the peccadiloes and condemnation of others. In short, a natural target for Uncle George. According to him her character had been warped for the want of a good man; 'Peabody ain't no good he's allus full o' beer an' that fancy chap can't be any good, or her wouldn't look so sour.'

But when she came into the baker's shop she looked more self-satisfied than sour, despite her severe appearance.

'And what do you think of your friend Kimmins and his daughter,' she announced. The remark was addressed to Uncle but was clearly meant to be heard by the customers in the shop. 'What's up now, Missus?' rumbled Uncle George.

The customers who were leaving suddenly decided there were other commodities they wished to buy. Mrs Peabody was obviously going to make a statement, Uncle George would be making some reply and it was not an exchange to be missed, even if it did mean buying an extra packet of tea or loaf of bread. There were several customers present, all of them women; Mrs Peabody had timed her arrival with care.

'You know as well as I do,' retorted Mrs Peabody.

'An' since when have you been interested in my opinion?' rumbled Uncle George, showing an unusual attention in attending to the wants of customers who did not appear to want their wants attended to in any great hurry.

'You are a particularly bad influence, and,' said Mrs Peabody, glancing round at everybody, 'everyone knows it, but even you surely cannot condone this disgraceful business of Kimmins' daughter, or his attitude.'

Uncle George ignored this, and continued to serve customers who seemed reluctant to be served, and who once served seemed even more reluctant to leave the premises.

'Now,' demanded Mrs Peabody, 'come on, speak up.'

'What's excitin' you, Missus?' said Uncle George, now giving her his complete attention to the evident relief of the customers.

'You know perfectly well what I'm talking about,' said Mrs Peabody. 'Kimmins' daughter, hardly seventeen, is expecting a baby. As you know, she's not married, that's bad enough, but what's even worse is that she's not going to get married. It isn't as if the father of the child is not free to marry her, he is and everybody knows he is. Any other father of a girl in the same circumstances would compel the wretched young man to marry his daughter. But not Kimmins, no, not Kimmins. I've talked to him, I've talked to the vicar to talk to him but all to no avail. Now, in desperation, I'm asking you to talk to him.'

'Why me?' asked Uncle George, all wide-eyed innocence.

'Because he's a friend of yours, he may listen to you. You've been a bad influence, now's your chance to be a good influence. I said to Mr Peabody –'

'I'll speak to Reuben,' said Uncle George.

'Good,' said Mrs Peabody and almost a smile appeared on her bleak face.

'I shall tell him as Mrs Peabody have been busying herself in summat what's no concern of hers an' what's no concern o' mine nor nobody else 'cept them as it do effect –'

'Oh,' gasped Mrs Peabody turning pale.

'But in my opinion, for what it's worth –'

'Ah,' said Mrs Peabody.

'If the girl don't want to marry the chap an' the chap don't want to marry the girl, then –'

'Quite, quite,' broke in Mrs Peabody.

''Tis a damned sight better they don't wed,' continued Uncle George.

'Oh!' gasped Mrs Peabody.

'An' what's more,' continued Uncle George, 'I shall tell Reuben an' his missus as they'm doin' the right thing by not forcin' 'em to get married against their will.'

'You wicked man!' said Mrs Peabody.

'I dare say you be right, Missus, but there's a sight –'

'And Kimmins is a wicked man.'

'No he ain't, nor his missus ain't; they'm good people an' they'll look atter their daughter an' the grandchild, which is more'n some o' they –'

'I've heard enough,' said Mrs Peabody, her face now bright red. 'The girl's a dirty slut –'

'Her ain't a dirty slut, her's as clean as a new pin.'

'I might have expected this attitude from you. I said to Mr Peabody –'

'You do me a great honour, Missus.'

'Honour, honour indeed. Everything about this whole business is completely dishonourable.'

'Have it your own way, Missus.'

The other people present had abandoned all interest in tea or bread. Wide-eyed; their attention was on Uncle George and Mrs Peabody.

'The baby will have to be adopted. I'll see to that!' said Mrs Peabody.

'Oh no, it wun't,' said Uncle George.

At this point the red-faced, irate Mrs Peabody may have made her escape but it was blocked by Uncle's erstwhile customers, she had no means of leaving easily and with dignity.

'But,' continued Uncle George, 'I'll tell ye what you can do as you be so keen on doin' things an' interferin' in other people's business what ain't no concern of your'n.'

As Mrs Peabody was more or less a captive in the shop she had to listen.

'When I was a boy chap we had a curate here,' said Uncle George, 'I mind as you an' some of the others here remember him, name o' Switchback – a funny name I allus thought – an'

he used to give us boys talks. Lectures, they was, there's allus
some what's keen on givin' lectures, Missus. For our good,
lectures allus be, that's why they'm allus so borin' an' why
nobody don't take much notice on 'em. But I remember one of
Mr Switchback's lectures. I wun't go into details, Missus, not
to embarass you nor nobody else, perticklerly meself, but
what he told us boys was if we came over all funny in a
pertickler place, to put'n under the pump. Now, I don't
reckon that chap o' Reuben's daughter knowed that an' you
know what happened.'

Uncle George paused. Mrs Peabody looked flabbergasted,
bereft of speech or action of any kind. The rest of the women
looked mildly shocked and averted their eyes from each other.
Uncle George on the other hand seemed completely at ease.

'And,' he said, 'If you was to make it your business – as you
make most things – to see as the young chaps today put theirs
under the pump – a proper job on't you understand, as it
would be if you had the handlin' on't, I'm sure – then these
happenings which you deplore wouldn't be so likely to occur.'

Crowd or no crowd, Mrs Peabody made her escape and did
not stop to hear Uncle George say, 'But there ain't no pump in
the spinney.'

*   *   *   *   *

'That interferin' 'oman,' said Uncle George to Father on the
following afternoon, as they sat down by the fireside. It was
Sunday, they were about to have a cup of tea, the prelude to
their usual discussion of the topics in the *News of the World*,
patent medicines and doctors. But this time Mrs Peabody took
precedence.

'And her allus up at the spinney,' said Uncle George, 'she've
got cause to talk about others.'

'She's talking about you,' said Mother coming in with a pot
of tea, 'and I don't wonder. She's told me and Mrs Gerrish
that she's off to see Mr Gummer, her solicitor, about those
malicious rumours you've been putting around about her.
Then you'll be in trouble.'

'Trouble, trouble, why trouble?' asked Uncle George.

'Because there's not a word of truth in it,' said Mother.

'If it ain't true, why did me bees go out o' their way to attack
her?' asked Uncle George.

'I expect it was because they're as vicious towards her as you are,' said Mother.

''Twas because bees don't like married women carryin' on with other chaps, they can't abide them capers, they most nearly allus go out o' their way to attack women what's at them capers. So naturally they –'

'Is that a fact, George?' asked Father.

'Stuff and nonsense,' said Mother.

'Oh, stuff an' nonsense is it, Ethel,' said Uncle George, 'Well, you just try carryin' on wi' some chap, an' I'll bet a dollar to a dime as they'll sting you black an' blue.'

'I've never –' began Mother.

'Here, steady on, George,' said Father, looking a little alarmed.

'I'm not stopping in here to be insulted,' said Mother. 'Why don't you say something, Father? How can you sit there and let him say such things?' She left the room quickly.

'What's his name, George?' asked Father.

'Who's name?' asked George.

'The chap who's carrying on with Mrs Peabody,' said Father.

'I'm not sure, but I believe it's Claude Piper,' replied Uncle.

Mother returned with a sponge cake. 'Here you are,' she said, slamming the plate down on the table, 'and I hope it chokes the pair of you.'

'George says it's Claude Piper, Ethel, who's a carryin' on with Mrs Peabody up at the spinney,' said Father.

'Never!' said Mother.

'I've got suspicions,' said Uncle George.

'Suspicions aren't evidence,' said Mother. 'Mrs Peabody and Mr Piper don't go to the spinney.'

'I don't say as they do, not at the moment,' rumbled Uncle George. 'It's bound to be dampish up there, just now. She'd be bound to catch a cold an' she didn't show no sign of one when she called in the shop yesterday for a bit of a chat. Most likely they've found somewhere dry for this time of year. With all the rain about they'd most likely have to.'

'Stuff and nonsense,' snapped Mother, 'a tissue of lies, wicked lies. Lies you'll pay for dearly after Mrs Peabody has consulted her solicitor. You've been at it for far too long, now you've gone too far. You'll be in serious trouble, you haven't a jot of evidence.'

'We'll see about that,' said Uncle George.

'Claude Piper,' said Father thoughtfully. 'That's a surprise, good living chap, regular church goer, high principles, well, well. Always seemed so strait-laced and respectable. . . .'

'That's nothing to go by,' said Uncle George. 'Remember Matthias Gooch, lay preacher, as strait laced and as respectable as you like. Allus talkin' 'bout principles, morals an' suchlike, teetotaller an' all. You remember how he used to go on 'bout the evils of fornycation. I don't hold with all that talk 'bout fornycation or interferin' with folk. If they wants to forny let 'em forny an' if they'm doin' wrong the bees'll get 'em. A good man everybody said, nobody ever suspected anythin' about him an' his housekeeper did they? Allus carryin' on 'bout others carryin' on, so nobody thought he was carryin' on with his housekeeper. An' if it hadn't o' bin for the burglar nobody 'ould ever ha' bin the wiser. That scared him, didn't it, an' he forgot hisself when he started tellin' the bobby an' one or two who happened to be with the bobby at the time. 'I heard a noise,' he said, 'and I sat up in bed, an' I heard it again an' I nudged my housekeeper – I mean I shouted my housekeeper . . .' But 'twas too late, he'd let the cat out o' the bag. An' he didn't go about lecturin' an' preachin' an' interferin' with folk no more atter that. And neither will Mrs Peabody after her cat's let out o' the bag.'

★   ★   ★   ★   ★

It was not long before most of the village knew that Mrs Peabody was going 'to have the law on' Uncle George. Reactions varied from concern to interest to jubilation. Father's, Aunt Aggie's, Reuben's, Colonel's and some others came in the first category.

'It looks black for you, George,' said Father, who was very worried.

'Black as thunder,' said Uncle, 'there'll be a storm.'

'I'm concerned about it, George,' said Reuben, ''specially after the way you spoke up for me daughter an' all.'

'Don't you fear none,' said Uncle.

'I'll give evidence for you, George,' said Colonel, 'you can depend on me.'

'Oh dear, oh,' said Aunt Aggie. 'Do you think they'll put you in prison?'

'I'm sorry, George,' said Dan Teakle, 'but I knew your tongue would get you into trouble one day. But if there's anything I can do.'

Mr Peabody showed mild interest, he went so far as to poke his head over the wall dividing his garden from the bakery yard to say, 'She's set on it, she's set on it.'

A few were jubilant, especially after Mrs Peabody's solicitor, Gummer, had been sighted in the village.

'It's the high jump for you at last,' said Micah Elford. 'I've a mind to see Gummer myself and tell him a thing or two you've said about me. With my evidence as well I reckon you'll get put inside.'

'You shouldn't have said such wicked things about poor Mrs Peabody,' scolded Mrs Gerrish. 'It's time it was stopped and I'm glad something's being done about it.'

'I'm surprised I've gone on letting you have papers and things,' said Mrs Hatch. 'I ought to have known – some of those things you read – Sexton Blake and murder, it's a wonder you haven't done something worse. I expect you would, given the chance, you've only been biding your time, you monster. All I can say is, I'm very relieved. Mr Gummer will stop us all from being murdered in our beds.'

It was not in the nature of Sam Fisher to be jubilant about anything, but he, too, added his comment. 'It was bound to come sooner or later. I've seen it coming for a long time, it's a wonder it ain't come sooner, but now it's come it'll all come out an' a lot more's goin' to come out than some expect. When he leaves the court, that is if they let him, he'll have a hand clapped on his shoulder and he'll be taken behind bars, and then later there'll be some very serious charges I shouldn't wonder.'

Mother oscillated between concern and jubilation before settling down to be 'worried to death', 'driven clean out of her mind,' and 'deeply disgraced.'

To all well-wishers and ill-wishers and to the curious, Uncle George gave the same reply; 'You can't keep a good man down.'

A second sighting of Mr Gummer in the village set tongues wagging with renewed vigour. Mr Gummer was a tall, thick-set, swarthy man with beetled brow and jutting chin. Like an evil bird of prey, observed Uncle George.

This second appearance of Gummer sent Father scuttling down to see Aunt Aggie.

'Our George don't seem worried,' he told her, 'but I'm worried to death.'

'Have a cup of tea,' said Aunt Aggie, 'and an aspirin, that's what I always give Sam when he's worried.'

Uncle Sam was sitting upright in his chair, the neck of his shirt undone. When Father refused a cup of tea, Aunt Aggie went to Sam, put her hand down inside Sam's shirt and began to scratch his back. 'I've been at this all evening,' she said, 'the poor old fella.'

'What are we goin' to do about bread, that's what I'd like to know,' said Sam.

'Oh bagger the bread,' said Father, 'what about George?'

'I'm going to see the vicar,' said Aunt Aggie.

'The vicar's going away in the morning for a fortnight,' said Father.

'Oh dear, and I can't go tonight, I've got Sam's back,' said Aunt Aggie.

'See Dr Higgins,' suggested Uncle Sam, 'get him to say George is of unsound mind.'

'Our George's mind is as sound as a bell,' snapped Father. 'Anyway, what's the matter with your back? If Aggie's got to keep on scratching it, you must be as lousy as a cuckoo.'

'You mustn't say that,' chided Aunt Aggie, 'the poor old fella suffers, he can't help it.'

'George, he won't see a solicitor, he says he don't want no truck with 'em. He says he can look after himself – dare say he's right, he's got a head on him like a lawyer. But I still can't help worrying. He won't worry, but I'm doing enough for the pair of us and to spare,' said Father, preparing to leave.

'It's a worrying time for us all,' said Aunt Aggie, still busily scratching Sam's back, 'all the way round, whichever way you look at it. If it isn't one thing it's another, there's no end to it. Now it's this terrible thing over George and Sam's back on top of it, it's all piling up, a heap of troubles. And the vicar going away, just when he's most wanted, it's too bad of him. You'll see yourselves out – slam the door really hard – I mustn't leave Sam's back.'

* * * * *

Three or four nights later we heard a church bell ring. 'That's funny,' said Father when we heard it again, 'it's not practice night, not unless they've changed the night.'

'I suppose you expect the bellringers to inform you first,' said Mother. 'But I should have thought you'd have had enough to worry you without worrying about bellringers, I know I have. It's the disgrace, it all rebounds on the family, especially me. At least I try, but it's a thankless task with the way that George . . .'

'There it is again,' said Father, cupping his hand to his ear.

'But at least he isn't here. I've been expecting him all the evening and dreading it. He usually comes Thursday evenings – still, I mustn't grumble, I'm grateful for small mercies.'

'There it goes again,' said Father. 'It's damned odd, just one bell and stop an' then again an' stop.'

Even Mother had to agree it was odd after we'd heard it again and yet again.

'I don't like the sound of it,' said Father.

'Perhaps it's a warning,' said Mother.

'Warning?' asked Father.

'They do say the end of the world is coming,' said Mother looking rather frightened.

'It's damned funny,' said Father, with hand still cupped to ear.

'Mrs Peabody was only saying yesterday,' said Mother, now looking thoroughly frightened, an emotion I was beginning to share. 'She was talking about the end of the world, when it had turned suddenly dark, it's all the wickedness she said. At the time I thought . . .'

'It's most unusual,' said Father, getting to his feet, 'I'm off to see what's up.'

'I'm not stopping here,' said Mother, 'just let me get my hat and coat.'

There were some people standing in the street, some looking through doorways, some peeping through windows. 'Summat's up,' Father told them. Some of them joined us, others withdrew and shut their doors. We met Alfred Tucker who asked what was going on. 'Summat's up,' said Father, 'and we're going to see what it is.'

'Good idea,' said Alfred Tucker, 'I'll come too.'

'Hurry up, Ethel,' said Father, 'there ain't a moment to lose.'

'I'm coming as fast as I can,' said Mother.

There were several people in front of us and more behind us, all making their way to the church where the bell was still ringing.

We met Uncle George. 'Summat's up,' Father told him.

'Ah,' said Uncle George, 'I was at Aggie's an' we heard the bell.'

'What d'you think's the matter, George,' asked Father.

'Oh, Sam reckons somebody's been and hanged hisself on a bell rope an' that's what's causin' the bell to ring,' said Uncle George.

'Oh dear,' said Mother, 'it's one thing after another, I can't stand much more of it. I don't want to see men swinging on bell ropes.'

'No bottle, the chap's no bottle, I can't see what our Aggie do see in 'im,' grunted Uncle George.

'I can't go another step, not at this pace,' said Mother. Actually our progress was very slow. Every few yards Father stopped, while he said 'Hark!' And every time we met someone we all stopped again to talk before moving on towards the church.

'Summat's up,' said Father.

'We'll know in a minute,' said Alfred Tucker.

We saw Colonel, Reuben and Arnold Ludgater. 'I've left the bar, I wonder what's going on,' said Arnold Ludgater.

'Summat,' said Father.

Mr and Mrs Gerrish were hurrying towards us. 'What's the matter?' said Mrs Gerrish. 'Why's that bell ringing? What are all these people doing?'

'It could be murder, arson, great balls o' fire, all manner o' things. We'll know directly. Whatever it is it have brought the village out,' said Uncle George.

'It's exciting,' said Alfred Tucker.

'It's damned silly, all these people rushing about, just because a bell's ringing,' said Arnold Ludgater.

'It's terrible, I can't stand any more of it,' said Mother.

'It's summat,' said Father.

'Old Sam wouldn't stir, not him,' said Uncle George.

'I read in the paper, they did this when the dam was bust an' no end of 'em got drowned,' said Colonel.

'Well, we ain't got a damn dam to bust an' drown us,' growled Arnold Ludgater.

'Well, that's a blessing,' said Mother. 'At least we've got something to be thankful for.'

'It's a pity the vicar's away,' said Mrs Gerrish.

'It would happen while he's away,' said Mother. 'That's always the way of it, just when you need somebody. If he'd been here, he could have said a prayer and perhaps it would have gone away.'

'We're here now,' said Alfred Tucker.

'I'm allus here wherever I be, 'tis a funny thing ain't it,' said Uncle George.

'I can't see anything funny about it,' said Mother. 'And for another thing, where's the policeman? He ought to be here. Still, it's always the way.'

'I'd aim he's miles away, kipping law an' order, on his bike,' said Colonel.

'It's not good enough,' said Mother, 'Going off at a time like this. He should be here, this is where we want law and order.'

By now we had reached the belfry. 'I'm going inside,' said Alfred Tucker.

'Do you think that's wise?' asked Father.

'It's locked,' said Alfred Tucker. 'Here – hold on – the key's in the door – now that's a funny thing.'

'Go careful, Alfred,' said Father.

'I'll come with you,' said Arnold Ludgater.

'Great balls of fire, swingin' men, ghosts, all manner o' things,' muttered Uncle George as Tucker and Ludgater went inside the belfry.

Four people came out of the belfry; Arnold Ludgater, Alfred Tucker, Claude Piper and Mrs Peabody.

'Well!' gasped Mother.

''Pon my soul,' said Uncle George.

'Well, I never!' said Mrs Gerrish.

Mrs Peabody looked distressed and confused, Mr Piper looked distressed and confused, every one else looked astonished.

'What's been going on? What were you two doing in there?' asked Arnold Ludgater.

'Fornycation,' muttered Uncle George.

'What's that? What's that?' said Mrs Peabody, recovering a little. 'What did you say?'

'Mortycation,' said Uncle George. 'It must ha' bin mortycation shut in there.'

'We've been in there for a couple of hours,' said Mr Piper.

'It was very dark . . .' said Mrs Peabody.

'We groped . . .' said Mr Piper.

'Did you, begod.' said Uncle George.

'Yes,' said Mr Piper, 'we groped and disturbed some bees . . .'

'They stung us,' said Mrs Peabody.

'That's the second time bees have gone for you, Missus,' said Uncle George, 'Bees do allus know an' they don't like it.'

'I shall have to go to the doctor,' said Mrs Peabody.

'Funny time of the year for bees to be about,' said Alfred Tucker.

'Funny business altogether,' said Uncle George.

'Funny place for bees to be,' continued Alfred Tucker.

'Expect they crept in there for the winter, out o' the wet,' rumbled Uncle George, 'like these two have.'

'How did you come to be in there?' asked Mrs Gerrish.

'I had a message about church business, urgent business,' said Mrs Peabody.

'A likely tale,' said Uncle George.

'So did I,' said Mr Piper.

'I didn't,' said Mrs Gerrish, tartly, 'and I'm always consulted about church business.'

'Funny place to have church business and only the two of you,' said Alfred Tucker. 'You don't usually have church business in the belfry.'

'Of course we don't,' snapped Mrs Peabody, 'but with the dear vicar away . . .'

'While the cat's away,' murmured Uncle George.

'I got here first,' said Mrs Peabody, 'then Mr Piper arrived and the door closed. We couldn't open it, it was locked, we were trapped.'

'We groped about in the dark,' said Mr Piper.

'And the bees stung us,' said Mrs Peabody.

'We waited, but no one came, we were in here a long time, being stung. We didn't know what to do,' said Mr Piper.

'Then Mr Piper rang the bell for help,' said Mrs Peabody. 'I shouldn't be surprised . . .'

'But you was surprised,' said Uncle George, 'both of you was surprised, the two of you alone together, if someone hadn't locked that door none of us would ha' known what was goin' on.'

'If ever I discover the perpetrator of this dastardly trick . . .'

'Dastardly trick,' said Mr Piper.

'Two highly respected members of the parish, it ain't good enough,' said Uncle George.

'I'll have Mr Gummer on to him,' said Mrs Peabody.

But Mr Gummer was seen no more in the village, and no more was heard of any action for slander. For some time after the incident in the belfry, Mrs Peabody's face went quite red every time the church bells started to ring.

Chapter Ten

In the Garden and in the Float

Easter, the time of blue skies, gentle showers and breezes soft as caresses, of white lacy plum blossom, lambs playing in orchards and little pigs rushing between the trees. A world of green fields; of chattering chain harrows and ringing rollers which turned the fields into alternating strips of light and dark green. The cuckoo came, in the woods were daffodils and wood anemones in flower, the latter more happily called windflowers. The time of salmon, elvers and turnip greens. A time when magic seemed to suffuse the air. Uncle George called it 'the sweet o' the year.'

The hot-cross buns had been baked, delivered and eaten, but it was no time of relaxation for Uncle George. The garden claimed all his spare time – and some of that which rightly belonged to the bakery business. Now, more than at any other season the bakery was an irksome business to him. Again and again he said he wasn't going to stick it much longer.

'You see those fields there an' that orchard,' he said, pointing to them one evening while we were in the garden, 'well, I ain't a coveteous man but I'd like them. And if they ever come on the market – which they most likely will afore long – I shall have 'em, I've set me heart on 'em. An' when I've got 'em I'll chuck the bakery business.'

The potatoes were all planted – the early ones, Arran Pilot, had been planted a month ago, the main crop, King Edward, had been planted on Good Friday, the traditional day for potato planting. We were busy sowing peas, lettuce, radish, onions, and beetroot – according to Uncle George, it just wasn't possible to have too much beetroot. Runner beans would be sown later; 'Never,' said Uncle George, 'put your kidney beans in until the laylack is in bloom.' We earthed-up the early potatoes, hoed the shallots and parsnips – Uncle grew a lot of parsnips in order to make wine. We admired the spring cabbage, broad beans and turnip greens. Broad beans and turnip greens were an essential part of his diet when in season. If more people ate more broad beans and turnip greens, he declared, there would not be so much illness about. 'Turnip greens and fat bacon,' he said, 'there's nothing to equal 'em except broad beans an' fat bacon.'

He always had a store of fat bacon as he killed two bacon pigs a year and as he only killed them when they were almost too big and fat to turn in the cot he always had a surplus of fat bacon. Whole sides, part sides of bacon which gradually turned green and rancid. Some of which he gave away, to Colonel and Reuben who appreciated it, and to Mother who did not.

'If,' she often said, 'he brings another great lump of that nasty, fat rancid bacon here, I'll ram it down his great, fat nasty neck.'

Uncle ate his fat bacon for breakfast, dinner, tea and supper, he had it fried or boiled, he ate it hot or cold. It was very salty so it had to be accompanied, and followed, by large amounts of cider; the rough cider he made himself from his own apples.

On Sunday mornings Uncle George also attended to his bees. At least, in theory he did, in practice they often got overlooked which meant queen cells and consequent swarming. And swarming meant a chase, with Uncle George banging on a tin tray. The ensuing tintabulation was supposed to cause the bees to settle, in theory if not in practice. It also established the ownership of the bees and gave the right to enter anyone's property in order to capture them. According to Uncle George. Micah Elford disputed this right. Argument raged between them and it seemed only a matter of time before the whole business would be before the High Court. Here Micah was at a disadvantage; Uncle George could reel off a list of eminent barristers, (could Uncle George know most of them personally? He talked as if he did), but Micah could only muster the names of two solicitors. One was Farquharson who lived in rather a grand Georgian house in the village. He was old, aloof and dignified, we saw very little of him but when we did he looked as brittle as bones and as dry as dust, and never spoke to anyone. A venerable figure indeed, but certainly no match for any one of Uncle's eminent and able men. Micah's other solicitor was Gummer, who held no terror for Uncle George.

If the bees had not been inspected by eleven o'clock, there was little chance that they would be inspected at all on Sunday mornings. At eleven or shortly afterwards Reuben and Colonel were almost sure to arrive and the rest of the morning would be devoted to discussion and cider drinking. Occasionally the Major joined the company at a quarter-past-twelve on his way back from church. Ostensibly he came to buy eggs, but his real reason was the company and the cider.

Major Mostyn had come to live in the village a few years earlier upon his retirement. His wife bred Dalmation dogs; great spotted muntle headed things, completely uncontrollable, Uncle said. The Major was a welcome visitor and listened with attention to everything that Uncle George told him. He admired Uncle's garden – 'it's absolutely marvellous, don't you know, the wonderful stuff you grow. I only wish I could grow stuff half as well, by jove, I do.' He was an enthusiastic gardener if not a very good one, and any small success he might have achieved was ruined by his wife's prancing dogs.

Nevertheless, he was undaunted and eager to learn. He constantly sought Uncle George's advice; and not in vain, Uncle George gave him constant advice on gardening. He read every book on gardening he could lay his hands on. 'I read in this gardening book,' he once said to Uncle George, 'that . . .' Uncle George held up his hand and said, 'You don't want to take no notice of what they do say in gardenin' books, Major. Tell ye for why, most nearly all on 'em be written by edycated men. No, I ain't got nothin' against edycated men – Mr Pontifex is an edycated man, an' a gentleman, an' I think the world on him an' he loves his piano, he's at it all hours of the day an' night. All alone he got nothin' else. I never let many days pass but what I go an' see if he's all right an' take him a few vittals an' suchlike. He's a lovely ol' man, most affable, a real toff. I keep an eye on him, look after him, 'cos he got no notion, an' I'll tell ye for why, he's edycated, see. Some say he an' his house is dirty, an' so it may be, but that's no matter an' he can't help it, all alone an' edycated. You mustn't judge people by appearance. Some be dirty 'cos they'm lazy, some be dirty 'cos they'm just dirty and some be dirty 'cos they don't know they'm dirty, some be dirty 'cos they can't help it, an' some be dirty 'cos they'm all alone. Take poor ol' Gert f'rinstance, she ain't dirty 'cos she'm dirty, she'm dirty, not like Mr Pontifex 'cos he's got none to care for him, Gert's dirty 'cos she's got nobody to care for. That's how men an' women be diff'rent, most women must have somebody to care for, most men must have somebody to care for 'em. Now me, I'm all alone, but I'm diff'rent again, an I tell ye for why, I'm an extr'ordin'ry man, you wun't find many like me. I can do most nearly everything an' most allus do.

'Now what was I tellin' you afore I told you that? Why, there's you, Major, if you was left to yourself a fair while you'd go as dirty as can be, stands to reason, an' no offence meant, but you be an edycated man, a gentleman, but unlike most on 'em you got the sense to seek sound advice an' I dare say, atter all, you wouldn't get really dirty, not filthy dirty. Not as it would matter if you did, you'd still be a gentleman an' I wouldn't like you none the less.

'I likes edycated men, but the trouble is with 'em they be so ignorant. Experts be the wust, they gets to know more an' more 'bout less an' less 'til in the end what they do know ain't worth knowin', even if anybody could understand what they was talkin' 'bout.

'But you be diff'rent, Major, you comes to live here an' gets to know us chaps an' pays attention to what we do say. When you want to know summat you comes to me an' you come to the right man, I can tell you summat what's worth knowin'. An' if you persevere, like you be doin', you'll grow marrers an' things what's worth growin'. Have another drop – I knowed you was a good chap the fust time I saw you drink a drop o' me cider, you can tell what a chap's like by the way he takes his cider.'

Alfred Tucker sometimes joined the gathering outside the garden shed. Then the conversation turned to fatstock and meat. If Micah Elford was spotted Uncle commented upon 'stinkin' ol' fish.' Local gossip, the weather, pigs and crops were other topics, but always, (in Spring and Summer when the group was at its largest), the talk returned to gardening. Especially when the major or Dr Higgins, another occasional visitor, was in attendance. The past, present and future of the village was discussed.

'This,' once said Dr Higgins, 'is like a village parliament.'

'I don't know what 'tis like,' replied Uncle George, 'but 'tis a damned sight more like summat than Winkleberry an' his parish council. You'd have a job to find a more footlin' lot o' nogmen. It's chaps like us what kip things to go. Dr Higgins, now where 'ould people be without him? You be a fust rate Doctor, that you be, Dr Higgins. An' the major, he's a furriner, but a fust class furriner an' there ain't many o' they, I'll be bound. An' Alfred's a fust class butcher, an' Reuben an' Colonel here, be fust rate all round chaps. 'Tis a pity Mr Bence don't join us, he's a fust class vicar – he don't go interferin' with folk, but if they wants help he's there like one o'clock. An' then there's me, well, I b'ain't a bad chap, bake a bit o' good bread, kip a few fust class pigs an' all, make a drop o' beautiful cider, give a bit of advice, grow some splendid vegetables an' generally kip things a goin' as they ought to go.'

Here Uncle George paused and glanced round at the company; Dr Higgins, Major Mostyn, Reuben and Colonel. The mug was refilled and passed from hand to hand. Dr Higgins said he must leave. Uncle George gave a sweeping gesture with both arms and said, 'I ain't finished yet, I'm goin' to tell ye why we an' a few others be good chaps –'

'Well, hurry up about it, George, there's a good fellow,' said Dr Higgins.

'I really must go,' said Major Mostyn rising to his feet.

'Here, hold hard,' said Uncle George. But the Major, making his apologies left.

'I ain't so sure about him atter all,' rumbled Uncle. 'I wasn't none too sure when I said it, but I included him out o' politeness just 'cos he was here. But now he's cleared off – in a bit of a huff if you ask me – I don't mind sayin' he's a funny un.'

'He's not a bad fellow,' interposed Dr Higgins. 'He's settled in here well.'

'Settled, be baggered,' said Uncle George, 'he can't settle nowhere no how, a flittin' here an' there, askin' questions. It was damned rude how he upped an' offed it. Fill his guts with my cider –'

'I don't want to offend you, George, but I'm a busy man –' began Dr Higgins.

'Of course you're a busy man, doctor, we're all busy men. Which is more'n you can say 'bout ol' Mostyn, but unlike him you're a civil man. And you wouldn't be such a busy man if you was to take my advice. I've got one or two new preparations an' a few old uns what you ought to consider using –' said Uncle George.

'Yes, yes, George,' said Dr Higgins, a little impatiently.

'I'm tryin' to tell ye summat,' said Uncle showing a trace of anger, 'but I shan't tell ye if that's goin' to be yer attitude.'

'Very well,' said Dr Higgins, resigning himself to another bout of Uncle's eloquence.

'I could tell you summat,' said Colonel.

'Shut up,' said Uncle, 'an' let me do the talkin'. If you don't want to listen to me I'll tell you summat. Instead of quattin' there an' quaffin' my cider you can do a bit o' diggin'. Now, what I was goin' to say – well, I don't know as I be now.'

'I'll be going then, if that's the end,' said Dr Higgins.

'It ain't the end, 'cos I ain't started yet,' said Uncle. 'What I was goin' to say is all on us be good chaps, now I'm sayin' some on us be good chaps. An' do you know why? I'll tell ye for why, it's because we all likes a bit o' gardenin'. There's nothin' like it, it settles your mind, it makes you content, it makes you humble, it gives you a sense o' wonder an' magic, all dried up bits o' seed, sproutin' an' growin'. And another thing, we ain't got no swank, I can't abide swank – never could. Now, that's the trouble with Mostyn, he've got bags on't. An' Alfred Tucker, he've got swank comin' to him – I can say it 'cos he ain't here – he've got swank. You ain't got swank, doctor, though you be a doctor. Now, I don't want to be rude, I can't stop listenin' to you all day, I've got to get off to me brother's.'

*　*　*　*　*

It was early on a Sunday morning in May when Uncle George received the message about the conger eel. Uncle George had been wanting a conger eel for some time and had made several requests to his friend down by the river. I'm not sure why he was so keen to obtain a conger eel, I suppose he just fancied a conger eel as a change from the eternal fat bacon. Whatever the reason, he had, as he said, got his heart set on a conger, and when a man's heart, especially Uncle George's heart – or perhaps more accurately his stomach – is set upon something, he will not rest contented until he has it.

'We'll be off directly,' said Uncle after he had told me about the conger eel. 'As soon as Colonel gets here. By all accounts he's a big un, a gurt monster of a thing. We'll have to take the float, it ain't been used for a while. I was hopin' Colonel would be here by now, there's a few bits an' pieces collected round it what'll have to be shifted first. We might as well make a start on't while we're waitin'. The garden will have to take a miss, the bees will have to have the go-by, but it can't be helped, you don't get the chance of a gurt eel every day of the wik. Freshly caught this mornin', very different from ol' Micah's stinkin' ol' fish what have bin hangin' about for days on end.'

The few bits and pieces around the float proved to be many bits and pieces – and some large bits and pieces at that.

'I can never understand how things accumulate,' said Uncle George. 'I've got no recollection of puttin' them there, 'tis my belief they puts theirselves there when you ain't lookin'. There's a lot of mysterious things what do go on what you don't understand, me boy, what even I don't understand, what nobody don't understand. Things you don't think about, but what wants thinkin' about and what I intend to think about when I got the time. Folk just don't think enough, I do my share to be sure, as much as I can, but t'others just don't pull their weight.

'Where can we put all this stuff? You can't chuck it away. It might come in handy some time. Now, that's another funny thing, not much of it ever comes in handy until you've chucked it away an' when you've chucked it away it ain't handy no more.'

'Now, I'll get in the shafts an' you push – right push – be you pushin'? Whoa, that'll do, we'll get the horse. Where's Colonel? The old nogman, he promised faithfully to be here on time. To tell you the truth, I'm gettin' fed up with Colonel with his dilatory ways, I'll bet it was him who hemmed the float in with all them muddles.'

The horse was harnessed, led out of the stable and hitched to the float. Then Uncle tied the horse's head to the gate. 'We'll just go an' have a look in the garden while we're waitin' for the nogman,' he said.

In the garden he stopped and looked round. 'There's a might o' work to do in here, but it can't be helped, I'm on all the time as it is. The Major will miss his cider this morning, he won't like that, but it'll do him good, he's gettin' too fond on't. Did y'see how he were knockin' it back t'other day? I'll lock the shed up, I don't want a lot o' gutsy chaps makin' free with my beautiful cider when I ain't here.

'Lord, there's a cloud o' bees, aimin' straight for the village, reckon they're atter Mrs Peabody, so that means she bin at it agen. Well, her would ha' bin, last night were Saturday night an' ol' Peabody would ha' bin in the Lion gettin' hisself half-cut. You can't blame the chap, you need to be half-cut half the time if you gotta live with her. But you'd think all they stings she's gettin' without a doubt would steady her up.

'Come on, we'll go an' see if that nogman's come. If he ain't we'll go without'n, but that gurt eel will take a bit of handlin'. I wish I could have got hold o' Reuben, he's a more reliable chap than Colonel.'

We found Colonel sitting in the float. 'Come on,' he said, 'I've bin sittin' here waitin' for you.'

'Waitin' be baggered!' exclaimed Uncle George, going red in the face and looking very fierce. 'Here we are, we've done all the work an' bin kickin' our heels up hangin' about for you, you gurt sawny nogman an' you have the impertinence to quat yerself in there an' say you bin waitin' for us.'

'The float's all covered in dust,' said Colonel.

'Of course it's covered in dust, it have bin in that shed doin' nothin', I can't understand how it is you ain't all covered in dust the little you do.'

'Are we goin' to get goin' or are we goin' to stop here while you go on bletherin' 'til the cows come home?' asked Colonel.

'Do you want any of that conger?' asked Uncle George. ''Cos if you do, I advise you to kip your mouth shut or you wun't have cause to open it for any.'

'This is goin' to be a nice outin' if you're goin' to kip on like this all the time,' said Colonel.

'We'll be off now,' said Uncle, getting into the float. 'No, we wun't,' he said, getting out of the float, 'here's old Charley, I must see to him, a drop o' summat in a bottle, a bit o' bacon an' a couple o' bob an' he'll be as happy as all the birds in the air. Lucky chap, Charley, got nothin', but as happy as can be, 'specially if he got a little summat.'

Charley, who now stood beside us, did not look particularly happy or lucky. Wearing a battered bowler hat green with age, a tattered coat and trousers too large, worn-out boots and with all his worldy possessions in a bag thrown over his shoulder, Charley looked 'down on his luck.'

Charley was one of several tramps who called periodically on Uncle George. Occasionally they performed some small service for him, usually they had some news to tell him and always he gave them a 'bit of summat.' It was the same with the Gypsies who came; there was always 'summat' for them. Uncle George had an affection for these travelling people, partly because he had a large and generous heart for all whom he considered down-trodden; but mainly, I think, because he admired and envied their free and easy life.

Mother called them 'rogues and vagabonds and ne'er do wells.' Most of the villagers thought much the same. But not Uncle George, they appealed to his romantic and rebellious nature, he was driven to anger by the way they were 'driven from pillar to post with every man's hand turned against them.'

When Charley had been given 'a bit of summat,' we set off in the float. 'Here, take the reins, me boy,' said Uncle George when we left the village.

'Have you ever thought of becoming a 'stainer, Colonel?' asked Uncle George.

'A 'stainer, George? I don't rightly know what a 'stainer is.'

'Give up the drink. Sign the pledge.'

'Can't say as I have, George.'

'No more have I. I've felt many temptations, but I ain't never felt tempted to sign the pledge.'

'It don't appeal to me, George.'

'I'm glad o' that, Colonel. So when we get back you wouldn't mind spendin' the rest o' the day collectin' dandelions. They wants pickin' now. You needn't bother 'bout stoppin' for tea, kip right on 'til the dew comes, your missus can help you.'

'I don't know about that,' said Colonel, hesitantly.

'Colonel,' said Uncle sternly, 'did you tell me a damnable lie just now, be you goin' to become a 'stainer atter all?'

'No, I b'ain't, George.'

'Well then, pick dandelions as fast as you can for the rest o' the day.'

'I'd rather do that than be one of they 'stainer chaps,' mumbled Colonel.

'That's settled then,' said Uncle George. 'When we get to that chap walkin' ahead of us, pull up, me boy.'

We drew level with the man and I did as instructed.

'Like a ride?' said Uncle to the man.

'I don't mind,' he replied.

'Neither do I,' shouted Uncle, 'Drive on, me boy.'

'You never gave him a ride,' said Colonel.

'No,' said Uncle George, 'let'n walk if that's his attitude.'

Eventually we came to the river and drew to a halt at a cottage on the river bank. 'We're here,' announced Uncle, 'safe and sound, hale an' hearty, fresh an' full o' fight. Stop here while I go to the door.'

While Uncle went to the door of the white cottage, Colonel said, 'He've got it on him this morning.'

We saw Uncle talking to his friend, an oldish man, tall and with white curly hair. They walked towards us, 'It's good on you, Wilf,' Uncle was saying.

'I've got him in the shed there,' said Wilf, pointing to a tarred wooden shed by the roadside. 'He's a big un, half a hundredweight at least – I couldn't ask you less than I did, but I couldn't ask you more neither.'

'Come on, Colonel, don't sit there, bring the float alongside this shed,' ordered Uncle George.

Wilf opened the door of the shed, and there on the floor lay a huge conger eel.

'Rajah rhubarb!' exclaimed Uncle. Wilf chuckled. Colonel just stared with his mouth open. I stared in amazement.

'Soak me bob,' said Uncle. 'What do you say, me boy? What do you say, Colonel? Say summat.'

'He's a big un,' said Colonel.

'Big un!' exclaimed Uncle. 'You look at a gurt monster like that an' say big un. Why, he's the gurtest monster of a thing a fella like you is ever goin' to see in all your born days an' you just say he's a big un just as if 'twere an extra sized worm or summat. If he was alive, he'd give you big un. He is jud, ain't he, Wilf?'

'He ain't moved since I dealt with'n,' said Wilf. 'And they takes some dealin' with. They're fierce, they'd have yer leg off. But I'm used to 'em, though I've never before had one as big as this, but I can deal with 'em. Now, you George, you ain't used to 'em, 'twould be useless you tryin' to deal with him if he was alive, you'd never master him, he'd have you, sure as eggs is eggs.'

'I can master most nearly everything, but damn my rags, I wouldn't want to tackle him if so be as he was alive, Wilf,' said Uncle George. 'Back the float up, Colonel. Look lively, don't stand gawpin' about, time's gettin' on an' you got a lot o' dandelions to pick. Open the door at the back of the float, you nogman.'

We struggled with the eel, Uncle puffed and quarrelled with Colonel, Wilf chuckled. Uncle kept saying, 'he's a gurt monster,' and eventually we got it into the float. We left Wilf chuckling by his shed and started on our return journey.

'He's a gurt monster,' Uncle said, over and over again. 'He's a gurt monster,' Colonel kept repeating until Uncle told him 'to say summat different or shut up.'

'The float do go well considerin' it ain't bin used for some while,' said Uncle.

'Could ha' done with a bit of cleanin' an' maybe a bit of grease,' said Colonel.

'Ah, an mebbe it would have had if you'd got there in time to do't,' growled Uncle.

I was handed the reins while Uncle George filled his pipe and looked at the eel. 'He's a gurt monster, he'll cut up into some grub, by God he will. There's enough there for me an' me brother an' his fambly, an' you, Colonel, an' Reuben, an' our Aggie – though I begrudge that Sam havin' any – maybe Dr Higgins 'ould like some, an' a few others what's deservin'.'

'Ah', said Colonel.

'Well, remember that while you're gettin' dandelions – we shall want a lot. All them as had our wine last Christmas will want double the amount next Christmas. Oh! did I tell you his name ain't Fenton at all, it's Frodsham.'

'Who?'

'Why, that little runt of a doctor what have come to live at Haycroft,' said Uncle George.

'You told me his name was Fenton,' said Colonel.

'I know I did, an' I'm now tellin' you his name's Frodsham.'

'Why did you say his name was Fenton, then?'

'I expect he called hisself Fenton at some time or other, those sort o'chaps have any amount o' names. Probably he was Fenton afore he got struck off.'

Uncle George took the reins again. 'What did he get struck off for, George?' asked Colonel.

'How do I know. Misconduct I expect, most nearly allus is.'

'What's that, George?'

'Could be all manner o' things, p'rhaps for killin' somebody, poisoned his wife, made a hash o' everything, allus drunk, allus fornying with his patients – they don't like that – medical council I mean, his patients might or might not, most likely not, I'd say, he ain't the sort most women 'ould like havin' fornyin' 'em, not from the look of 'im. But I don't know what he've done, I can't be expected to know everythin'. I ain't heard much about 'im really, I'm just going by the look on him, which ain't nice . . .'

'Hey up, George!' said Colonel.

'Now, what's the matter?'

'That conger, he's movin', he's –'

'Course he ain't, Wilf have seen to 'im, he's as dead as mutton.'

'Why's he openin' his mouth an' showin' his tith, then?'

'Nonsense.'

'Now he's movin', look yerself an' you'll see,' said Colonel.

The reins were handed to me. 'Begod!' exclaimed Uncle, 'The bagger's alive.'

'I told you.'

'Look at that gurt mouth, look at them tith,' said Uncle. 'He's alive, Wilf must have only stunned him. Begod, if I had summat I'd stun the gurt monster good an' proper.'

'You ain't got anythin',' said Colonel.

'I know I ain't. Begod! The bagger's rarin'! Look at his tith! Begod, instead of us yuttin' 'im, the bagger's goin' to yut us! What can us do!'

Commotion reigned in the float. Uncle set about the conger with his stick. That made matters worse by enraging it. It lunged at Uncle. Uncle grabbed Colonel as if he was a shield. Colonel kicked and swore, Uncle waved his stick and swore. The horse began to take fright, I was terrified. Uncle lost his hat, Colonel almost lost a leg, luckily it was no more than a trouser leg which he did lose.

What with the terror, shouting, the angry eel and general panic and rumpus, I'm not sure what happened next. Not until Uncle George shouted, 'Open the door Colonel, an' we'll try an' shove the bagger out.'

The door at the back of the float was opened; fortunately the conger eel seemed as eager to part company from us as we did from it. The eel slithered out and flumped in the road.

'Good riddance to him,' said Uncle.

'That were a near go,' said Colonel.

'I'd gone right off him anyway,' said Uncle George.

'I'd got as I didn't like'n very much,' said Colonel.

'Mind, mum's the word about this little job,' said Uncle
'You know what folk are an' how they do talk. Nobody knows
about it except us three an' if we kip mum nobody else will
know.'

'What about Wilf?' asked Colonel.

'It's five miles down to the river and anyway Wilf don't tell
nobody his business, but I'll pop down and see'n during the
wik, just to make sure. Besides, it'll give'n somethin' to laugh
about for many a long day when he's sittin' by the river.'

Two or three days later there were reports that a large
conger eel, weighing at least a hundredweight, was seen about
a mile and a half outside our village. The reports were met
with disbelief at first, but then there were more sightings. No
one could understand how the creature had managed to get so
far away from the river. Uncle George, Colonel and I kept
mum and it remained a mystery. But as Uncle George said,
some people do exaggerate.

Chapter Eleven

At the Show

Mother did not want me to go to the county agricultural show with Uncle George. No good will come of it she warned, no good ever comes of anything with which that cratur's connected. He was, she said, filling my head up with a lot of rubbish – giving me those Sexton Blake stories to read – when I should be filling my head with learning, and if I must read, why couldn't I read books like *Tom Brown's Schooldays*.

When she learned that Mr Timms was also going to the show with Uncle George, she relented. Mr Timms was a respectable man, he kept himself to himself and did not drink.

'At least there will be no rowdyism and drinking if Mr Timms is there,' she said. 'He'll be a good influence. I wish you saw more of Mr Timms, he'd help you with your schooling. Then you'd get on, even get to college, perhaps, and get a nice respectable job and I'd be so proud. I know George is your uncle and that you're very fond of him, but. . . . But it's drink, drink, drink. Nothing but drink, well, drink and several other nasty things. I wish your father wouldn't go to that dreadful Lion with him – I stop him as much as I can – but when he does go with that George he always comes back so silly. If there's one thing I hate more than another it's drink, drink and drunkenness and other nasty things, and goodness knows we see more than enough of all of them with that George. But with Mr Timms there'll be none of that.'

She might not have agreed if she'd known that Reuben and Colonel were also coming. 'It'll be a bit of a squeeze in the back,' said Uncle George as he pushed Colonel and me and then Reuben into the back seats. 'We shall have to let Mr Timms sit in the front seat as he's a pertickler kind o' chap.'

'Why's he coming?' asked Colonel, 'it ain't as if you do have much to do with him.' It was obvious that Mr Timms was not entirely welcome as far as Reuben and Colonel were concerned.

'Mr Timms likes a show, that's why he's comin',' said Uncle.

'I dare say there's lots what like's a show, but that don't mean we've gotta take 'em all with us,' grumbled Colonel.

'If you don't want to come, Colonel, there'll be more room for them as do,' said Uncle George.

'Of course I want to come, or I wouldn't be here now.'

'Well then, shut up an' kip a civil tongue in your yud an' be polite to Mr Timms when he's with us,' instructed Uncle.

Mr Timms was waiting outside his house at the far end of the village. 'So kind of you to take me,' he said as he got into the seat beside Uncle George.

'We're glad to have you,' said Uncle. 'We're pleased you're coming with us, aren't we, me boy?'

'Yes,' I said, and so I was, pleased that Mr Timms was going with Uncle George. Without him I may not have been going either.

'Ain't we, Reuben? ain't we, Colonel?'

'Yes' said Reuben.

'Oh yes, very much so, absolutely delighted,' said Colonel, 'when I learnt as you was comin', I was that pleased, why, –'

'That'll do, Colonel,' grunted Uncle, 'Mr Timms ain't daft nor deaf – he heard and understood you the first time, there's no need to go on about it an' monopolise the conversation. That ain't bein' polite, that's bein' ignorant. Mr Timms most likely wants to say summat, ain't that so, Mr Timms? You'd like to say summat?'

'It's all very nice, very nice indeed, oh yes, very pleasant and very kind, very good company, I've a feeling I shall enjoy myself today,' said Mr Timms.

'An' so you will, Mr Timms, so you will, an' so shall all on us,' said Uncle George.

'I got rid of my little motor, now I'm retired I don't really need it. Oh useful, useful, I grant you, but the amount I used it didn't really justify the expense. You must look at all these things. I'm a great believer in that, giving everything some thought,' said Mr Timms.

'Quite right, Mr Timms, you're a man after me own heart. You're a thinkin' man, a wise man,' said Uncle.

Mr Timms gave a nervous little laugh and said, 'I wouldn't say that, I've done some foolish things in my time.'

'Ah, but I'll warrant you've done your foolish things in a wise way,' said Uncle.

And with more pleasant conversation like this we made our way and eventually arrived at the show.

Mr Timms was tall and thin and stooped slightly, he had long white hair, rather sharp features and horn-rimmed spectacles perched on his prominent nose. Today he was dressed in a dark suit and had a white rose in his buttonhole. During the journey I learned that he had spent a lifetime in insurance, had a wife who was rather delicate, two married daughters and three grandchildren, that growing roses and playing chess were his hobbies.

Once we were in the showground he informed us in his precise voice that there were a few things he wanted to see, most of which were in the flower tent.

'That's all right, Mr Timms,' said Uncle George, 'you go your way and we'll meet later. I've got rather a lot to get round so you wander round on your own. But don't overdo it, with all I've got to see and do I shall be pretty tired by the end of the day and I most likely will be much obliged if you'll drive us home.'

Mr Timms assured Uncle George that he would be most happy to oblige, that he was a most careful driver, he had not spent a lifetime in insurance without learning the wisdom of driving carefully. But first, before visiting the flower tent he would like to see the animals, but – and he scarcely liked to presume on Uncle's kindness any further – he would be most grateful if Uncle would accompany him and give him the benefit of his knowledge.

'Of course, of course,' said Uncle George, 'it would be a great pleasure, because to tell you the truth, Mr Timms – although I've never known you really well and have never been in your company much – I've taken a great liking to you. You're a man after me own heart, 'pon my soul, if you ain't.'

'Oh,' said Mr Timms, 'I am most obliged, most obliged. And I take it very kindly, the things you have said. I really am quite flattered, I really am. After your own heart, well, well, that's very nice. What a pleasant day we are having to be sure.'

We went and strolled slowly up and down the cattle lines. Uncle George with much wrinkling of his brow, puffing-out of cheeks and gesturing with his stick, discoursed upon each breed in turn. From him we learned that; Gloucesters were a good old general purpose breed, regrettably neglected, but until they became popular again there was little chance of getting good cheese. Friesians were dismissed as some foreign breed and hardly worth our attention, Guernseys were all right for what they were, but not a breed he would choose. Ayrshires were all right for them as liked them. Jerseys were pretty little animals that gave rich milk but were far too bony. The dual purpose Shorthorns and Red Polls were the breeds he'd choose, should he ever happen to go in for milking. Beef Shorthorns, Devons and Sussex were topping breeds for beef but no breed when it came to beef could hold a candle to the Hereford.

The various breeds of sheep were dealt with quickly, but, he assured Mr Timms, if he, Mr Timms, should ever go in for sheep he would not go far wrong if he kept Kerries, Rylands or Suffolks, but which ever breed should happen to take his fancy it was most important that he used 'a Suffolk tup on 'em.'

'Quite so, quite so, I'll remember that,' said Mr Timms, gravely nodding his head.

It wasn't until we came to the pigs that Uncle George waxed eloquent and enthusiastic. A long time was spent gazing at the Wessex Saddlebacks, an even longer time and discussion was spent over the Gloucester Old Spots. 'There is,' said Uncle George, 'nurn a fairer breed, they're the sort to keep, Mr Timms. You know, you're just the man to keep pigs.'

Looking at Mr Timms, he did not seem just the man to keep pigs. But that was only my opinion and what was my opinion compared to that of Uncle George, when it came to pigs and the right sort of man to keep them. Mr Timms however, seemed to share my opinion. 'I don't think,' he began.

'No,' said Uncle George, 'it probably ain't occurred to you. But now I've explained to you, you will. You're a thinkin' man, same as meself an' you'll go home an' think. An' what'll you think of? You'll think of pigs, same as me, I think a lot about pigs. I dare say I'm about the most thinkin' man o' pigs at this show today.'

'Well, well,' said Mr Timms, 'perhaps I shall, life's full of surprises – you learn that in a lifetime of insurance.'

''Pon my soul, Mr Timms, you never spoke a truer word, nor no other man ever have. Life is full o' surprises an' you'd be surprised at the number of surprises I've encountered in me lifetime.'

'I would not be at all surprised,' said Mr Timms.

'Bless my soul, Mr Timms, you've done it agen, you be a surprisin' man. But you've spoke the truth, soak me bob if you ain't. There comes a time when a man gets full o' surprises an' he ain't surprised no more. Really, Mr Timms, gettin' to know you as I be gettin' to know you is a surprise in itself. In fact I'm surprised I ain't got to know you better afore. All as I can say is as you're most excellent company an' it'll be a great pleasure to put you in the way o' pigs.'

Mr Timms beamed with pleasure.

'Colonel have got a good eye for pigs,' said Uncle George. 'You ought to get better acquainted with Colonel, Mr Timms, he really is a splendid fellow. An' Reuben, you ought to chum up with Reuben too, he can put you in the way o' poachin' an' so on. You strike me, Mr Timms, as a chap what would fancy a bit o' poachin'. Yes, yes, both of 'em are toppin' chaps, I don't know where I'd be without 'em.'

After a brief inspection of the horses, we parted from Mr Timms after arranging to meet him later by the secretary's tent. As we watched Mr Timms making his way towards the flower tent, Uncle George said, 'He's a good chap, a most superior person, we ought to see more of him than we do, he's got a longish old head, he has.'

'Ah,' said Colonel.

'Ah,' said Reuben.

'Now,' said Uncle George, thumping his stick on the ground, 'we've got a lot to do. Come on.'

After a few yards we came to a feeding-stuffs merchant's booth. 'In here,' said Uncle, leading the way. A man spoke to us. 'Interested in your pig food,' said Uncle George, 'as I keep a lot o' pigs an' I've heard good reports of your stuff.'

'Come and sit down, sir, and have a drink while I tell you about it. Now, what would you like?'

'Whisky,' said Uncle George. 'An' these two chaps are my pig-men, they likes beer – proper pigs for beer they are, so bring 'em large glasses on't. An' me nephew, he'd like a drop o' lemonade.'

When the drinks were brought, Uncle was told about the merchant's pig food and asked how much of it he'd like to order.

'I'll have to think about it,' Uncle answered and then as an afterthought, 'Thirsty work, thinkin' – oh, thank you, another wouldn't come amiss. What do you say, chaps?'

When the second lot of drinks was finished, Uncle said he thought a couple of ton would do for a start, but on the other hand it might not be enough, he'd give it further thought – no, he wouldn't stop now, he'd let them know in a day or two.

We left the booth but soon entered another, also a feedstuffs merchant's. Uncle said much the same as he'd said in the first and with the same results. It was the same again in the adjoining booth.

'It's goin' well, ain't it,' said Colonel.

'Nice drop o' beer,' said Reuben.

'We mustn't waste our time,' said Uncle George, marching ahead. Twenty yards on was a merchant who specialised in poultry food. Here Uncle George enquired about pheasant food. 'This is my gamekeeper,' he said, jerking a thumb towards Reuben. 'His young pheasants ain't doin' as well as he'd like – he's very pertickler y'know – an' we thought maybe we'd give your'n a trial – oh, about half a ton for a start – oh, that's very kind of you, whisky for me, beer for my chaps and lemonade for my nephew – yes, we're all got a bit peckish –'

As we left, Uncle was given a card with the merchant's name and address which he put in his pocket with the cards he'd received from the other merchants. As he did so he said, 'Well, I've got your telephone number, I'll give you a call to confirm the order – no, no, don't book anything definite, when me an' my gamekeeper have talked things over we might decide to have a ton instead.'

'Good bit o' cheese, wasn't it,' said Reuben, as we were standing outside while Uncle George was wondering which way to go.

'Reuben ain't your gamekeeper, nor you ain't got no pheasants, leastways not yet, an' most likely you wun't 'ave 'til just before Christmas,' said Colonel.

'I know that,' said Uncle, suddenly walking at a swift pace towards a fertiliser merchant's booth.

'Can I interest you in any of our fertilisers, sir,' said the merchant.

'Oh yes,' said Uncle George.

'Perhaps you'd like to step inside and take some refreshments, sir.'

'That's uncommon civil of you, a bit to eat an' a drop to drink would suit us all round.'

Refreshments were brought by a waitress, Uncle introduced Colonel as his foreman, Reuben as his cowman and implied that he, Uncle, had quite a sizeable farm.

'What kind of fertilisers are you interested in?' asked the merchant.

'Pig muck,' said Uncle George emphatically, 'you can't beat pig muck, it's got body in it, not like these artificials. I don't hold with them, they ain't no bottle.'

'Yes, yes,' said the merchant, rather taken aback, 'I don't deny pig manure has got its uses –'

'I should think not,' said Uncle sternly.

'But,' continued the merchant, 'we all realise you must use artificial fertilisers –'

'I wouldn't have 'em on my place; blood an' bone an' suchlike's all right, slag's useful stuff, but chemicals ain't no bottle.'

And with that Uncle stumped off out in a great state of indignation.

'First Reuben's your gamekeeper, then he's your cowman, I can't understand it, it ain't true,' said Colonel.

'Of course it ain't true,' said Uncle George. 'It's all lies. As you know I b'ain't in the habit o' tellin' lies I only tells 'em to those as like 'em. Some 'ould rather hear lies than the truth, I only tell 'em to oblige. All these chaps I've told 'em to today have been as pleased as punch, they wouldn't have been half so pleased if I'd told 'em the truth. Y'see I like to make people happy, an' there can't be anythin' wrong in makin' people happy.'

'That man in there, you didn't make him happy,' said Colonel.

'No, I don't think I did. And do you know for why? It was because I told him the truth. Which just goes to prove what I've bin tellin' you,' said Uncle.

We came to a stand exhibiting poultry houses; after a thorough examination of every house, Uncle ordered two and we were all given a drink.

At another stand Uncle George ordered three pig huts and again we all had a drink.

We strolled along the rows of machinery, Uncle ordered a mowing machine at one stand, a horse rake at another, a plough at another, then a dung cart. And with each order there were whisky, beer and lemonade.

Then Uncle George showed a great deal of interest in tractors on a stand. 'I don't know,' said Uncle to the salesman, 'if these things will ever catch on. I prefer horses meself – oh, this is me nephew an' these two chaps are a couple o' me carters. Givin' 'em a day out, damn good chaps. Here, what do you chaps think o' these here tractors?' Getting no response from Colonel or Reuben, Uncle George said to the salesman, 'They do love their horses. Well, and I do, but –' Here Uncle paused, rubbed his nose and wrinked his brow. 'As one o' the leading farmers in my district, I feel I've got to be progressive – set an example – lead the way as it were – and, I don't know –'

'Have a drink, sir, and have another look,' said the salesman.

'Oh, very kind of you – a drop of whisky if you've got some. My men prefer beer, damn good chaps, both of 'em can handle horses, none better. Yes, a drop of beer would suit 'em very well, but not in fancy little glasses, both of 'em are very pertickler about things like that – comes of allus bein' with horses, horses be very pertickler animals.'

The salesman was at pains to show and explain every detail of the tractors.

'I don't know,' said Uncle George very slowly. 'For meself I'd have one like a shot, 'specially as I'm increasin' me acreage very shortly, but – well, you've got to consider your chaps, 'specially when they're damn good reliable chaps. I'll tell you what, we'll have a stroll round an' I'll see if I can talk 'em into it.'

In a corner of the showground, we came across a group of men, each one of whom had pound notes tucked in the brim of his hat, thrust in the top pocket of his coat and clutched in his hands. They were all waving their arms, prancing about and shouting, 'Money, money, money.'

'Hullo,' said Uncle George, coming to a halt, 'here's a rum business an' no mistake.'

'Money, money, money,' they shouted. One of them I then noticed was darting about with an upturned hat in his hand. Two more appeared and joined in the chant, 'Money, money, money.'

'I wonder what their game is,' said Uncle, 'whatever 'tis it's a swindle of some sort.'

'I've never seen anything like it,' said Colonel.

'We'll stop an' watch their antics an' see if we can fathom it out,' said Uncle.

'I wonder who they are and what they're up to,' said Reuben.

'They're wrong uns an' they be up to summat,' Uncle said loudly. Most people were ignoring the men and walking quickly past.

'We'll stand our ground,' said Uncle George.

'I don't like the look of 'em, nor the way they're lookin' at us,' said Colonel.

'We'd better move on,' said Reuben, 'it's no business of ours.'

'I'm makin' it my business,' said Uncle. 'Damned swindlers, the lot on 'em.'

'They're lookin' at us,' said Colonel.

'One of 'em's comin' over,' said Reuben, 'let's move off.'

One of the men sidled up to Uncle George and muttered, 'Ever felt the razor, Guv?'

He then started to move away, Uncle George slipped his stick between the man's legs causing him to stumble and fall. Three or four of his companions moved menacingly towards us. 'Time to get on,' said Uncle George, breaking into a trot. We all scampered away and the men, fortunately, didn't follow.

'That was a near go,' said Colonel.

'I felled the bagger,' said Uncle George.

We kept moving at a sharp pace, with occasional glances behind, until we came to a booth advertising cattle medicines.

'I got to go in here most pertickler,' said Uncle George. And once inside he began to order packets and bottles of medicine by the dozen.

'Ah,' said Uncle to a delighted salesman, 'whisky for me, beer for me chaps and lemonade for the boy.'

After further examinations on some dozen stalls, which included much stick prodding and many criticisms of the products from Uncle George but no orders, he announced it was time we went in search of Mr Timms. 'Begod!' he exclaimed as he looked at his watch, 'I didn't realise the time had gone on so much. He'll be waitin' for us most likely.'

Most probably very likely, as it was long past the time we had agreed to meet him. And there he was, patiently waiting by the show secretary's tent.

'There you are, Mr Timms,' said Uncle George. 'We've been searching all over the place for you.'

'I did begin to wonder if I had been waiting in the wrong place,' said Mr Timms. 'I am so sorry if I have inconvenienced you.'

'Think no more of it, Mr Timms, think no more of it,' rumbled Uncle George as we walked out of the showground.

'The car's this way,' said Colonel.

'That's what I like about Colonel, Mr Timms, he allus knows where things are,' said Uncle.

'I expect you have had a busy day,' said Mr Timms.

'A helluva busy day,' said Uncle, 'it's tired me right out, Mr Timms, I'd be most obliged if you'd do the driving.'

'Of course, of course, a pleasure, the least I can do,' said Mr Timms.

'To tell you the truth, Mr Timms, I feel a bit drowsy. I've had a few drops of whisky. Oh, I didn't want it, it was forced on me, every few yards out would come an arm an' drag me into a booth. And once inside, they'd insist on givin' me a drop an' I don't like to offend people.'

We had travelled several miles when Uncle George said, 'I hope you don't mind me sayin' so, Mr Timms, but you ain't as good a driver as I thought you'd be.'

'I am a little out of practice,' said Mr Timms.

'I shouldn't think you made much of a job on't when you was in practice.'

A little colour came into Mr Timms' normally pale face, but he said nothing.

'You'll pardon me,' said Uncle, 'but I don't much care for the way you double de-clutch.'

Nothing more was said until Colonel asked if we could stop for a minute. Colonel, Uncle George and Reuben disappeared behind a hedge.

'Right,' said Uncle when they returned. Several more stops had to be made later.

'Reuben an' Colonel have trouble with their bladders,' explained Uncle. 'It's on account of 'em allus working in the open in all winds and weathers.'

'It's been quite a day,' said Mr Timms.

'Quite so, Mr Timms,' said Uncle George. 'Now, I hope you'll pardon me, but are you a 'stainer?'

'No, I am Church of England, but I don't go very often.'

'I'm glad of that, I've got no time for those fancy religions. But Church of England's all right, it stops a man gettin' too religious an' interferin' with folks. It don't stop women of course, but it's women's nature to kip interferin' an' nothin' can stop 'em. But you mistook my meanin', what I meant was are you teetotal?'

'No, no, I have an occasional glass of sherry, but I do not normally indulge, only on special occasions,' said Mr Timms.

'In that case you'd have no objection to stoppin' at that pub yonder – they keep a drop o' good beer there,' said Uncle George.

'Not at all, not at all,' said Mr Timms. 'In fact, I would like a small glass of beer myself.'

'Would you, Mr Timms, would you now.'

'You see,' said Mr Timms, 'it has been a special occasion for me today.'

Fifteen minutes later we continued our journey. 'Tell me, Mr Timms, as you're a thinkin' man, I expect you do a lot o' readin',' said Uncle.

'Only detective stories, I'm afraid. Sherlock Holmes is my favourite,' replied Mr Timms.

'Well, well, but it don't surprise me, no, not a jottle. I like Sherlock Holmes, Mr Timms, and 'Sexton Blake.'

'Sexton Blake, I've not ready any since I was a boy.'

'I've got a great stack on 'em, Mr Timms, you're welcome at any time.'

'Most kind, most kind,' said Mr Timms.

Again the years of work in all winds and weathers effected Colonel and Reuben and Uncle George. As we waited, Mr Timms said, 'Your uncle is a remarkable man.'

When we were almost home, Mr Timms said, 'I have been thinking over what you said about keeping a pig.'

'I knew you'd come to it, Mr Timms, a man like you was bound to. I'm not surprised, but I am surprised how quickly you come to it. You are a wonderful quick thinker, I'll be bound. Reuben will soon knock you up a little cot, I'll put you in the way on it an' Colonel will give you a hand any time you want it.'

'Pig manure is so good for roses,' said Mr Timms.

As we parted from Mr Timms at his house, Uncle George said, 'You should come an' join us on a Sunday mornin' in the garden shed, Mr Timms. It's just your sort o' company, we're all gardenin' an' thinkin' men an' we have some very high class talk.'

★   ★   ★   ★   ★

On the following evening Uncle George was very busy writing letters cancelling his orders of the previous day.

Chapter Twelve
Uncle George's Courtship

It was a mellow evening in July, the air was suffused with the scent of honeysuckle and lime blossom; the sound of birdsong, the murmuring of innumerable bees and the tune of crickets. This, the stillness of the world, the dappled shadows on the ground, the benevolent sun itself, lent enchantment and the promise of magic to the evening.

It was a Tuesday evening, a time when it would be almost certain that Uncle George would be in his garden and alone. For me, these were the best times, these summer evenings with just Uncle George and me in the garden. I would help him with his work, and as we worked we would talk, man to man. His opinion would be given, mine would be sought, each of us would listen attentively to the other; good solid talk it would be. At these times, Uncle George would be at his most fascinating and endearing and at his most lovable.

On Tuesday evenings he was usually all alone, Reuben and Colonel would be playing skittles, Alfred Tucker would have been to market and after market safely installed in the Rose and Crown. Even Micah Elford was usually too busy to look over the hedge and start an argument. On Tuesday evenings after we had finished working in the garden, we would sit by the garden shed, the cider mug would be filled and shared, a companionable silence would be shared. And then Uncle George would say, 'I remember . . .'

On this Tuesday evening Uncle George was pulling some early beetroot when I walked into the garden. With his back still bent, he turned his head and looked at me and, with a lovable smile upon his red face, said, 'Hullo, my boy.'

When he had a sizeable bunch of beetroot in his left hand he straightened his back and said, 'I'm sorry, me boy, but I must go and get washed and changed, I've got to go out for a bit.' With no further explanation he bustled off, only pausing to tell me I could weed the onions if I'd got a mind to. But weeding onions without the company of Uncle George soon proved a dull job.

It was much the same on Friday evening, except that this time I met Uncle George by the entrance to his house. He was freshly shaved and smelled of soap and was wearing his best suit and hat, and had several beetroot in a basket. 'Hullo, my boy,' he said. 'I'm in a bit of a hurry, 'fraid I can't stop, I'm just off out.'

Again there was no explanation, which was odd and rather distressing. Was I not Uncle George's best friend, had he not repeatedly told me so himself; and so often he had said, 'I'm tellin' you, me boy, 'cos there's no secrets between us, but mum's the word.'

On Sunday he came to lunch as usual and seemed his usual self, except for his well-shaved face. After lunch he sat in an easy chair, drank cups of tea and discussed topics in the *News of the World*. But not at length, and doctors and medicines and local gossip were not discussed at all. In fact, he left very early, saying he had to be off, he must go and see to his livestock.

'What's the hurry, George?' asked Father, 'it's early yet.'

'Time goes on,' replied Uncle George enigmatically, 'and six o'clock will be here afore I can look round.' And he left without any further explanation.

'Deuced odd, our George rushing off like that, without a word,' said Father.

'He's shaved and he's cleaner, now that's odd,' said Mother.

'But rushing off like that.'

'That's a relief, we must be grateful for small mercies.'

'I don't like it. Not like our George,' said Father.

'I do,' said Mother.

'Pour me another cup of tea, Ethel, old lady.'

On the next Tuesday evening I found Uncle George in his kitchen. He was standing in front of the looking glass brushing his wool-like hair. Again he was freshly shaven and wearing his best suit. On the table stood a basket with beetroot.

'Hullo, me boy, you've caught me at an awkward time, I'm just going out.'

My face must have shown my disappointment and puzzlement, because he told me in a gentle voice to sit down a minute.

I sat down at the table, Uncle sat on the other side, between us stood the basket of beetroot. 'I'd better tell you summat,' he said. I nodded and bit my lip, Uncle's voice was so quiet and serious.

'We've never had no secrets from one another, not you an' me, boy, an' we wun't have now. Allus been friends, you an' me and allus will be.'

Again I nodded, not knowing what was to come, and not trusting myself to speak. It was all very odd; constant shaving, best suit, always going somewhere and always taking beetroot. All innocent things in themselves but – well, I feared the worst, although what that was I did not yet know. And now I was about to know. . . .

'But,' Uncle George continued, after a slight pause, 'mum's the word.'

Uncle and I were too old and fast friends for me to feel the need to give a verbal or any other promise to keep mum or for him to expect it. I had never divulged any of Uncle's secrets. And Uncle for his part had never broken any promise he had given me.

'I have been thinking,' he said, 'in fact I have been giving the matter some thought for some time, on and off. Here I am, not gettin' any younger, hale and hearty mind, fit as a fiddle, apart from a few twinges, a touch o' wind an' suchlike – but I've got remedies to counteract them, an' they're bringin' new uns on the market all the time. Then o' course, there's Higgins' mixture, that's a good stand-by – although, as I've told him times out o' number, he could do a lot more for others if he'd only use some o' the remedies I've recommended.

'But on the whole I'm fit as a fiddle – as I need to be, mind, workin' in all winds and weathers all hours o' the day an' night. I eat well, not to kill meself as some on 'em do, but I eat well an' I drink for me stomach's sake, not to make a pig o' meself like some, but in good moderation. But, when all's said, I b'ain't gettin' any younger. And, here I am, all by meself; nobody to look after me, nobody to cook me grub, nobody to greet me when I get back, bathered out after a hard day's work. Aggie do come an' do a bit o' dustin' an' suchlike, but she ain't gettin' any younger either. An' she've got that ol' Sam, an' if that ain't enough to make an old woman of her I don't know what is.

'Of course I manage all right, I ain't got nothin' to grumble about. But the time might come, not for a long time I grant you, I got a wonderful constitution, but these things have got to be faced. An' 'tis no good leavin' 'em to the last minute. In my experience the last minute is most allus too late anyway.

'I could look round and try to find a housekeeper, I might be lucky enough to find a good un, on the other hand I might not. At first I thought that might be the best thing, but the trouble with housekeepers is you've got to pay 'em.

'Well, that was that, an' that might ha' bin the end on't, if it hadn't bin for that nice little widder woman what have come to live about here. Mrs Williams is her name, a very nice superior woman. Every time I delivered her bread, allus the same, tidy an' affable, oh, a charmin' lady. A few years younger'n me – an' that's no disadvantage. Allus, come inside – manners, see – an' a cup o' tea an' sometimes a slice o' cake, made by herself an' damn good. Not gushin' or pushin' or over familiar, nothin' o' that kind, friendly, but keepin' herself to herself at the same time, if you understand me – just as a lady should. Nice an' tidy, good furniture, everything what do denote a superior person. Good cook too, I never smelled cookin' like it.

'Well, boy, there was the answer, starin' me right in the face every time I took bread to her house.'

Uncle George paused and fiddled with his pipe. 'The long an' the short on it, boy,' he continued, 'is I've decided to get wed. I'm callin' on Mrs Williams some evenin's a bit, takin' her a few beetroot. She's very partial to beetroot. But mum's the word, boy, for a time. Give it another week or two to see how it do go. Then I'll tell your father, he ought to be the first to know. Then there's Aggie, when I give you the word, you can tell her.

'Of course, it'll be all over the place in no time at all, but I can't help that, nor it ain't no matter. But not for another week or two, I'm still in the early stages an' nothin' bin said between us. No, that ain't the way to do't at all, I shan't say nothin' outright to Mrs Williams, I'll be very delicate. Mrs Williams will respect that way o' goin' on, her bein' a lady. We'll have a quiet wedding, just fambly an' mebbe a drink at the Rose – the Lion wouldn't be suitable for a lady like Mrs Williams. But, for now, boy, mum's the word.'

★   ★   ★   ★   ★

Soon Father was told of the courtship and I was sent to tell Aunt Aggie.

'Courting is he?' said Aunt Aggie, 'Well, I hope it's somebody suitable this time.'

'At it again, is he,' said Uncle Sam. 'At it all the time if you ask me. Never stops, I reckon. And how many this time – well, it'll all come out in time, these things always do.'

'What's she like?' asked Aunt Aggie, 'I don't get out much, I don't meet these new people, I don't know what's going on most of the time.'

'An' a good job as you don't,' said Uncle Sam. 'In my job I see enough an' more'n enough, an' soddem and goodmorrow ain't nothin' to what I see or hear tell on. When I'm decoratin', 'specially at some o' them furriners' houses I kip a wary eye an' even then, why, some of them women 'ould be at me, arms all round me, a kissin' an' a huggin' if I wasn't careful.'

'Oh Sam, you poor old fella,' cried Aunt Aggie, 'I had no idea it was as bad as that.'

'It's a proper job with some of 'em,' said Sam gloomily.

'Oh, you poor old fella,' said Aunt Aggie in distress, 'no wonder you suffer so with your poor old head.'

'They can't come their wiles with me, I'm too sharp for 'em,' Uncle Sam said.

'Of course you are, Sam, you dear old fella,' cried Aunt Aggie, 'but it's too bad, they shouldn't do it, but perhaps when they look at you they can't help it, poor things.'

It was not long before Uncle George's visits to Mrs Williams were known generally. The courtship progressed. Uncle stopped coming to us on Sundays, instead he went to Mrs Williams. And when he did visit us he extolled the excellence of her cooking.

'Her dumplings, Ethel, are absolutely A1. Now yours allus gave me a touch of the wind. She's got a light touch with pastry, you're a bit too heavy handed, Ethel, I allus think. And her sponges, they slip down a treat; yours are all right, Ethel, but occasionally they ain't cooked enough.'

'You ungrateful wretch,' said Mother. 'All the years you've eaten me out of house and home, while I've worked my fingers to the bone, filling that great cannister of yours. If you ever eat another piece of my cake in this house, I hope it chokes you.'

'Steady on, Ethel, old lady,' said Father, 'don't upset yourself, our George never meant any harm.'

'Well, I did,' snapped Mother leaving the room quickly and near to tears.

Uncle George began taking Mrs Williams to the cinema every week. He even washed and polished his motor car every week. There was a trip to the seaside one week, the theatre the next. Uncle George's garden began to show signs of neglect, the beetroot began to dwindle.

Reuben drew his attention to the serious consequences of a beetroot shortage. 'What about beetroots for wine, George? Think of next Christmas.' But all that Uncle said was that Mrs Williams was very partial to beetroot.

Colonel also expressed concern about the beetroot. Both he and Reuben had shared in the proceeds from last Christmas's wine trade and hoped to do so again next Christmas.

'Why don't you take her a bunch o' flowers instead, George,' he suggested.

'Flowers,' said Uncle George, 'that 'ould be a fine thing, a man in my position walking down the street with a bunch o' flowers.'

'A box of chocolates then,' said Colonel hopefully.

'Chocolates, be damned,' said Uncle. 'Every time I take her to the pictures it's a box o' chocolates, an' chocolates ain't half dear. Besides, Mrs Williams is very partial to a beetroot.'

Mrs Williams was brought to meet Father and Mother.

Father said afterwards that he thought she was a very superior little woman. Mother said she was a dowdy, dumpy little thing, much older than she pretended to be and she, Mother, could not see how anyone with hands like Mrs Williams could possibly be a good cook. Her hands had apparently not been worked to the bone and never would be, she would never work from morning to night filling George's great stomach and keeping him in comfort. Not that he would ever discover it because Mrs Williams did not want him and never would have him.

'I thought,' said Father, 'that she seemed fond of him, the way she looked at him. They'll make a splendid match.'

'I am not sure,' said Mother, 'which is the softest, you or that great hulk of a George.'

'This is it, after all these years,' said Father, 'our George is goin' to wed and settle down, you'll see.'

'He'll be back, he'll come back, bad pennies always do. And before I can turn round and know where I am he'll be eating me out of house and home.'

Mrs Williams was also taken to meet Aunt Aggie. Aunt Aggie liked her, I learned a few days afterwards, but she was not sure whether she was quite the woman for George. Uncle Sam expressed no opinion on Mrs Williams; his only observation was that he had seen it all before. What he had seen before was never explained.

Reuben thought she was 'a bit stand offish,' Colonel thought she was 'a bit posh.' But neither Reuben's nor Colonel's opinion was without prejudice. Both viewed with dismay the dwindling amount of beetroot in the garden. Both resented the curtailment of the Sunday sessions in Uncle George's garden. As usual they arrived at eleven o'clock, but instead of staying until a quarter to one as they used to, they were curtly told to go at half past eleven.

'Come on, you chaps, I want you off the ground now, I've got to be at Mrs Williams' in half an hour.'

I will not venture an opinion of my own as I, too, could hardly be impartial. I did not dislike her, in fact I rather liked her – but she had come between Uncle George and me. In appearance she was of medium height, had brown hair with a few strands of grey – she was probably about forty years old – and well dressed in a quiet way. Her manner towards me was friendly but rather reserved.

On his infrequent and fleeting visits, Uncle George usually said something which upset Mother.

'Mrs Williams has got a beautiful new costoom, Ethel. You ought to get to know her better, you could learn a lot from her about how to dress, you ain't got much idea as it is,' he said on one occasion.

After he had left, Mother said, 'He only does it to hurt me.'

'I'm sure he doesn't mean any harm,' said Father. 'And anyway, I'll buy you a nice new costoom, you'll need one for the wedding, it's bound to be this fall the way things are going.'

Next we heard from Mrs Peabody that Uncle George and Mrs Williams had been to church on a Sunday evening.

'That,' said Mother, 'show's that she' no lady. Ladies go to church in the morning, not the evening.'

Soon, however they did start going to church in the morning instead of the evening. 'That won't suit George,' said Mother, 'no Sunday dinner. This will mean the end of their little business.'

It did not, however. We used to see them walking up the street on Sunday mornings as the church bells rang. Uncle George in his best suit, on his best behaviour and with a flower in his buttonhole; Mrs Williams beside him, dressed in what we thought must be 'the beautiful costoom.'

'I wouldn't put it on my back,' said Mother. 'And look at that great George making a bigger fool of himself than he's ever done before.'

'I know it's awful, I know I shouldn't, but I can't help laughing,' was Aunt Aggie's comment upon Uncle's regular church going. 'He never used to like it, Mother had an awful job to get him to go to Sunday School.'

This regular Sunday morning attendance at church meant the end of those jolly meetings of gardening and thinking men in the garden. But, Uncle George, perhaps mindful of the neglect of the garden, now spent Sunday evenings working in it. Reuben and Colonel, disgusted at the turn of affairs, refused to help. But at least it meant that I had Uncle George all to myself on Sunday evenings. 'You're a good boy to help your uncle,' he said. 'And very different from them who's only use was guzzlin' cider. Ill-bred varmints, I'm sorry to say – I shall have to give them the cold shoulder in the future. Yes, I'm afraid there's some on 'em as'll have the go by.'

The weeks went by, the visits to Mrs Williams continued; the beetroot in the garden grew, but the more it grew the less there was. Nobody could imagine what Mrs Williams could be doing with all the beetroot Uncle George took to her. Colonel and Reuben thought perhaps she was making wine, but I think that can be discounted. Uncle George said she was very partial to beetroot and so he took her some almost every time he visited her. After all, he'd said many times in the past it just was not possible to have too much beetroot.

The village, all of us, got used to Uncle George's courtship. Even those who had had doubts about the suitability of the match came to regard it as inevitable.

'It'll be nice to see George settled with a wife. And if they're not quite suited now they'll grow to suit in time, I expect. Oh, I know I shouldn't, but I can't help laughing, – George, with a wife,' said Aunt Aggie.

'I'm glad he's getting married at last, perhaps he'll stop all that soddem and goodmorrow business – it ain't no good to nobody,' said Uncle Sam.

'Well, I suppose it's all for the best. At least he looks and behaves in a more respectable way. And he won't be forever here, eating me out of house and home and worrying me clean out of my mind. We must be thankful for small mercies and count our blessings,' said Mother.

'Our George'll make a toppin' husband, you see if he don't,' said Father.

'Well, it's the end of all we've known, it'll be different now, but it were good while it lasted, we've had some fun together,' said Colonel.

'He allus said you couldn't keep a good man down, but it seems to me he've downed hisself an' the lot on us with him,' said Reuben.

'Poor little 'oman, chuckin' 'erself away on the likes o' him with his nasty ways,' said Micah Elford.

It was all just a matter of time. Mrs Peabody said she would let Mother know as soon as the banns were called, but there would be no music at the wedding, she would see to that.

★   ★   ★   ★   ★

We had almost grown accustomed to the absence of Uncle George at Sunday lunch. And when he arrived at about twelve o'clock on a late September Sunday we were all surprised. It was Mother who saw him first. 'Here's that George, and he's coming here,' she said.

'Our George, begod!' exclaimed Father.

A slightly unshaven, a rather unkempt Uncle George – in fact the lovable Uncle George of old, the one with a mischievous grin and a twinkle in his eye – came into the living room.

'Why, it's our George,' said Father.

'Of course it's George,' said Mother.

'What brings you here, George?' asked Father.

'I've come for a bit o' dinner, if you can spare a bit,' replied Uncle.

'Spare a bit, spare a bit,' said Father. 'Did you hear that, Ethel, old lady?'

'I did. I suppose I'd better peel some more potatoes,' said Mother, 'and start working my fingers to the bone to fill that great canister.'

'There, there, George. Ethel's all afire to get you some grub,' said Father delightedly.

'Some things are too good to last,' said Mother going to the kitchen.

'You didn't come down to the garden, my boy,' said Uncle George. 'Nor Colonel, nor Reuben. I waited an' none o' you came. It's unaccountable an' most unreliable the way some on you do behave.'

'I thought you would be at church with Mrs Williams or at her place,' said Father.

'No,' said Uncle George. 'I've had me fad out with that caper.'

'Why's that?' asked Father, 'I thought you were set on gettin' married.'

'I ain't set on't no more,' said Uncle George.

And no more was asked or volunteered until after lunch. When the meal was over and Father and Uncle George had settled in easy chairs, Mother brought a pot of tea.

'Well, George,' she demanded, 'let's hear the rights of it.'

'I've said afore an' I'll say it again,' said Uncle George, 'you don't know where you are with women, they be so strange, fickle creatures. Yesterday evening I went to see Mrs Williams as have been my custom of late. I took her some lovely beetroot too. "Oh George," she says, "I'm so glad you've come, I've got someone here I want you to meet," an' in she takes me to her drawin' room an' who should be in there but that little runt of a doctor fella, Frodsham what lives at Haycroft.

'After introducin' us she asks us to excuse her a moment an' out she goes. Frodsham, he was more of a runt than I thought he was, an' there he sat, squint eyed an' shifty.

'"I hear you don't do no doctorin' now," I says to him, hopin' I could wise some o' his guilty past out o' him. "I've never done any doctorin' in my life," he says. Oh, I thinks to meself, he've done summat wuss than ever I thought, he's as guilty as can be or he'd never have said that.

'If he thought he could get away with a trick like that, he had another think comin', I thought. "If you've never done any doctorin' why do you call yourself a doctor?" I said. "Because

I am a doctor of philosophy," he said, lookin' about as perky as a little shifty eyed runt can look.

'Ah, I thought to meself, you con't know the manner o' man you're dealin' with yet, I ain't bein' put off the scent with fancy words or poor old ruses like that.

'"But you cut people up," I said to him, an' thought to meself an' cut 'em up in little pieces no doubt. "No, no, no," said the runt, tryin' to brazen it out.

'Oh, I thought, to meself, perhaps poison was your little game was it. So I said, "If you weren't a surgeon, you must have been a physician, give folk medicine an' suchlike." The little bagger just sat there, trying his best to smile, so I thought I'd make it easy for him.

'"Gave some on 'em a drop too much, or the wrong stuff, bit of a mistake like, easy done I suppose. Dare say it happens more often than we know, all hushed up – expect it's got to be, otherwise there'd be panic or summat."

'"Look here, my man," he says, rising to his feet, but that didn't make no difference, he's such a runt he weren't no taller when he stood up. "Look here, my man," he says again – now if there's one thing more than another what puts the hell in me, it's when someone calls me his man, I ain't nobody's man but me own. But I let that pass, I wanted to get to the bottom of his little business. Then he says, "I'm not a medical man, I'm a professor, a university lecturer."

'"Why are you allus here then, never at university?" I asked – that I thought would set him back. But no, it didn't, he's crafty an' no mistake, used to bein' cross-questioned I suppose.

'"Because," he said, nice as ninepence, in that shifty way o' his, "I am on a sabbatical, I am staying here to write a book on philosophy."

'That, I must admit had me stumped. And I couldn't pursue the matter because Mrs Williams returned carrying a tray with sherry and glasses. But I don't intend to let the matter rest, I'll start makin' enquiries first thing tomorrow mornin'.

'"Oh," she says, as cheerful as a cricket. "I'm so pleased you two are getting on so well. Now, we'll all have a glass of sherry. Dr Frodsham and I have a little secret, we want you to be the first to hear. George, Dr Frodsham and I are going to be married."

'I was flabbergasted, didn't know what to say. She was smilin' an' that little runt was smirkin' for all he was worth, which ain't much, I'll warrant. It was a bit of a shock but me wits rallied as they most allus do an' I wished 'em luck. An' begum, she'll need it with that shifty little runt round her. I left as soon as I could, the more I looked at him, the less I liked'n. But I'm surprised about her, I thought she was a sensible little 'oman, but she's as stupid as the rest on 'em.'

'Begod,' said Father, 'I've never heard the like on't.'

'I am sorry, George,' said Mother.

'There's no need to feel sorry, Ethel,' rumbled Uncle. 'I b'ain't sorry – to tell you the truth I'd had more'n enough on't, 'twere makin' an old man o' me. All that shavin' wasn't doin' me face any good. All that dressin' up, them stiff collars – they was chokin' me. All that goin' to church, that weren't doin' me any bottle neither. I never could abide it, no sooner be you sat down but what you gotta stand up an' once you're standin' you gotta start kneelin'. An' all that gallivantin' about; pictures an' chocolates an' that were an expense. An' no time for me garden an' pigs an' me friends.'

'Ah, George,' said Father, 'you're well out on't. You be lucky to be shut of her an' the whole job.'

'I know I be,' rumbled Uncle George, 'I feel a great burden have been taken from me, I'm as happy as all the birds in the air. I can get back to me proper business o' livin'.'

'Begod, George, you're right, you've no cause for regrets at the way things have turned out, begod, you ain't,' said Father.

'I have, I've got one regret,' said Uncle George.

'Have you, begod,' said Father looking surprised, 'an' what's that, George?'

'It were a terrible waste o' beetroot,' rumbled Uncle George.